Teaching Your Children Responsibility

Linda and
Richard Eyre

A Fireside Book
Published By Simon & Schuster
New York London Toronto
Sydney Tokyo Singapore

FIRESIDE
Rockefeller Center
1230 Avenue of the Americas
New York, New York 10020

First Fireside Edition 1994
Published by arrangement with Deseret Book Company
Previously published as Teaching Children Responsibility

FIRESIDE and colophon are registered trademarks
of Simon & Schuster Inc.

Manufactured in the United States of America

10 9 8 7 6 5 4 3 2

Library of Congress Cataloging-in-Publication Data
Eyre, Linda.
[Teaching children responsibility]
Teaching your children responsibility / Linda and Richard Eyre.—1st Fireside ed.
p. cm.
Originally published: Teaching children responsibility. Salt Lake City, Utah : Deseret Bk. Co., © 1982.
"A Fireside book."
Includes index.
1. Responsibility. 2. Children—Conduct of life. 3. Child rearing—Religious aspects—Mormon Church. I. Eyre, Richard M. II. Title.
BJ1451.E97 1994
649'.7—dc20 *93-40139*
CIP

ISBN: 0-671-88716-5

Contents

Preface to the Third Edition

Why are there hundreds of parenting books about babies, toddlers, and preschoolers—and hundreds more about adolescents and teenagers—yet practically none about elementary-school-age kids, those between the ages of four and eleven?

Is it because preschoolers and adolescents are more difficult?

Because parents worry more about toddlers and teenagers?

Because babies are small and the mistakes of teens can be huge?

Probably all three of these reasons are true. But if we're thinking about *opportunities* to teach rather than about *problems* to solve, elementary-school-age children are excellent subjects.

At this age, kids can grasp concepts and understand principles that preschoolers can't, yet they do not have the skepticism or cynicism of adolescents. From both the standpoints of mental capability and emotional acceptability, four- to eleven-year-olds are *teachable.*

They are flattered by responsibility.

They are motivated by praise.

They are old enough to take initiative yet young enough to take suggestions.

They learn quickly from their mistakes, and at this age their mistakes will not kill them.

The elementary school years are a window of opportunity during which you can teach your children to be responsible for their *things,* for *work,* for their *actions,* for their *talents* and *potential,* for their *character,* and for their *choices.*

This book is probably different from other parenting books you may have read. It will help you act rather than react. Most parenting books take a problem-oriented, somewhat negative approach. They say, for instance, "If you have this problem, try this technique to solve it." Or, "If Johnny does this wrong, you can react by trying that." The implication is the parents are only capable of reacting.

Actually, the biggest problem parents have is that too often they are just reacting to what their children do, instead of assuming responsibility for the situation, taking control, and *acting* as parents. If parents have no clear or specific objectives for their parenting, all they can do is try to react properly. But if they have clear goals in mind in terms of what they want to teach their children, they can act, they can take the initiative, they can gain control of their family's destiny.

This book is designed to bring results! It is based on the objective of teaching children responsibility. It subdivides the objective into twelve types of responsibility, and offers proven methods by which they can be taught to elementary-school-age children. It suggests that you concentrate on one separate form of responsibility each month during the year.

This is a personal book. It is not written as a textbook, nor as "teacher to student" or "expert to novice" advice. It is written *parent to parent.* Our main credential is our experience as parents and our desire to be better parents. Stories, incidents, and personal experiences make up much of the book because we, like all parents, have learned through experience. We have also been able to draw on the experiences of the thousands of other parents who belong to our national parents' co-op, HOMEBASE.*

We've included more than 200 different, proven methods for effectively teaching responsibility to children grade-school age and younger. Read the book like a menu: Pick the kind of responsibility you want, turn to that chapter, and choose the methods that will work for *your* children.

When *Teaching Your Children Responsibility* was first published in the eighties, it sold 40,000 copies within the first few months. When our book *Teaching Your Children Values* was published in 1993, it sold over 300,000 copies in the first few months and hit number 1 on *The New York Times Book Review* bestseller list.

What was the difference? Are "values" more important or better sounding than "responsibility"? No. The nineties are a better *time.* Parents are more concerned, more committed, and more involved in parenting than they were in the eighties.

Raising children in the nineties is an awesome challenge. Parents are ready and willing to meet that challenge, but today's parents need—and deserve—all the help they can get. We hope you'll find help you can use in this book.

—Linda and Richard Eyre
McLean, Virginia
Fall 1993

---

*If, after reading this book, you decide you would like a more structured curriculum for teaching your children responsibility and values, you may want to become a member of HOMEBASE. If so, please see our postscript and the response card at the end of the book.

Introduction: To You as a Parent

It's frightening to raise children in the nineties. We know it and you know it. We share a certain bond as parents, and, unfortunately, part of that bond is worry. We worry about our children's physical safety. We worry about their emotional and social safety. We worry about the adequacy of their education. We worry about the effect of the indulgent, convenience-oriented, leisure-emphazing society we live in. We worry about the amorality and the increasing absence of standards surrounding our children. We worry about the whole range of uncertainties that lie in their future.

Our parental instinct is to *protect.* And we try to do so in all sorts of ways. Some of us install security devices or give our children training in abduction avoidance. Some of us struggle to afford private education, and some remove children from schools to educate them in the home. Some of us regulate what our children watch and listen to. Some form elaborate trust funds to secure their children's financial future. Some move to rural communities in attempts to give them deeper roots and basic values.

Deep down, however, regardless of what we do, we know that the only real and lasting way to protect our children is to teach them to be responsible for themselves. You probably picked up this book because you realize that. We wrote it because we realize it.

For us, the frightening aspects of parenting began to become evident about the time that our older children started school. Up until then, we had struggled with the typical highs and lows, the joys and frustration of preschoolers; but our worries had been mostly confined to whether they were healthy and happy. With school came a whole host of other worries. The stark reality hit: Our babies had begun the irreversible process of moving away from our influence and control and toward times and situations when their destiny would be more and more controlled by others' influence—and by whatever influence they would gain over themselves. We began to realize that we had to do more than "give them a fish"; we had to teach them "how to catch fish." We began to feel the need to teach them responsibility.

One day during this period, we had a rather simple experience that opened to us a new perspective on parenting. Richard had spent the day in his management consulting office with the owner of a small business who was experiencing various difficulties. Richard didn't realize just how serious his problems were until he asked him, "What are your *objectives?* What are you trying to do with this company?" He looked a bit dazed and replied that he wasn't quite sure. "My objectives?" he said. "Well . . . to make a profit, I suppose."

As an adherent of "management by objective," Richard spent the rest of the morning helping him clarify his goals and assuring him that once he had clear, specific, realistic ideas of what he wanted, he would almost certainly find ways to achieve it. As with other similar cases, Richard couldn't help feeling a little critical of a man who gets involved in something without much idea of what he wants to do with it.

That man's problems and others that followed made the day a hard one, and as Richard drove home that evening he found himself anticipating a simple, calm evening at home with Linda and their three small children.

Simple? Calm? When Richard got home, he learned that the three-year-old had broken a carton of eggs (one egg at a time) on the kitchen floor, and that before Linda could clean up the mess, the baby had slipped in it, hurting his nose. The five-year-old was complaining that the kids in kindergarten had been mean to her and she was not going back. Linda was making her best effort to stay calm and not quite succeeding. The frustration level was high and got higher when the baby found a broad-tip permanent marker that the three-year-old had separated from its cap. We spent the evening cleaning up, scraping off, comforting, and generally struggling.

Finally, when the children's sleep rescued us from them,

we sat down to catch our breath, and Linda said, "What are we trying to do with all these kids?"

The connection might have slipped by if she hadn't used the same words Richard had asked in his question to the problem client that morning at the office. "What are we trying to do?" In other words, what are our objectives?

So we tried to answer the question. And our response was as general and vague as that of the failing businessman. "Our objectives? Well, we're trying to rear them, that's what; to bring them up, to guide them."

Richard's critical words of that morning now turned on him. "If you don't have a clear idea of your specific objectives, you'll end up reacting all the time, instead of acting. If you want to succeed, you need some precise goals. How can you get so involved in something with so little idea of what you want to do with it?"

It was the beginning of a new approach in our family, one of "parenting by objective." As we thought about it over the following days and months we realized that many of the frustrations and failures we were experiencing in parenting had to do with the fact that we didn't have any objectives or yardsticks with which to measure our performance. Since we had no specific goals, we tended to evaluate our parenting on momentary feelings, which were often exasperation or lack of patience or other negative emotions that made us feel negative about our parenting.

We decided that we needed objectives, not only for our own fulfillment and peace of mind, but for the success of our marriage, our family, and our children. We decided that if we had clear objectives for what we wanted to give our children we would be able to *act* more and *react* less. We decided that, without goals, we had been on the defense too much. We decided that perhaps the best defense was a good offense.

Over time, we concluded that the best objective for small children was *joy*—that in the impressionable preschool years, children with the right guidance could expand their capacity for various kinds of happiness. We decided that, for children under five, JQ (Joy Quotient) was more important than IQ (Intelligence Quotient). We subdivided "joy" into thirteen different categories and wrote a book for parents called *Teaching Children Joy*.

However, as mentioned, our real worry started with our elementary-school-age-children. And we knew, as all parents must when they think about it, that the objective should be to teach children *responsibility.* They can start learning it before they start school. And if they haven't basically learned it by the time they finish elementary school, the chances are that they never will.

What does it mean to teach a child responsibility? If you were to ask ten parents, you would probably receive ten different answers. To one it might mean teaching a child to make his bed and put his pajamas away. To another it might involve motivating children to do family jobs or to take their share of household work. Some parents may want to teach children responsibility simply because it would lessen their own work load, giving them more time and more freedom.

In the context of this book, *responsibility* means more than any of these—far more. It means to become mature in the sense of being responsible *to* family, *to* self, *to* society. It means being responsibile *for* all aspects of our lives and our situations: for our talents, for our potential, for our feelings, for our thoughts, for our actions, for our freedom.

Responsibility is not the result of maturity, but the cause of it—and a major responsibility of parents is to teach responsibility.

On its most basic level, responsibility is obedience. At its next higher level, it becomes morality or care for how our actions and attitudes affect others. Then it becomes discipline. Then, at its highest level, it becomes service.

Children best learn responsibility through this sequence. They learn first to be responsible to their parents (obedience); then to be responsible to society for who they are and for what they do (morality); then to be responsible to self (discipline); and finally, to be responsible to and for other people (service).

Very small children can grasp responsibility as it applies to obedience, to things and to certain kinds of work. As they grow, they can feel responsibility for their actions. More maturity can bring responsibility for choices and character, gifts and potential, and finally responsibility for other people.

The earlier levels of responsibility prepare a child to accept the later levels. The sequence of responsibility can best be understood in diagram form:

Age	*Responsibility as:*	*Responsibility for:*	*Responsibility to:*
6 or younger	obedience	obedience things work	parents
8	morality	actions talents and gifts peaceful attitude	society
10	discipline	choices character potential	self
12	service	family dependability contribution	others

Attempting to teach responsibility out of sequence is hardly ever successful. It is difficult for a child to feel responsible to society if he has not previously learned responsibility to his own parents. A child usually cannot understand responsibility for his talents or potential until he has accepted responsibility for his actions and for his possessions. Understanding discipline is much easier for a child who understands obedience.

The ages on the chart are general and approximate. Different children can grasp and gain different forms of responsibility at different ages. What is important is not the precise age, but the *sequence* in which responsibility levels are taught. The first concepts should be taught to children as early as they can handle them and should be followed by the succeeding sections in sequence.

So much for theory. Starting with chapter 1, this book becomes a method book, with sections corresponding to the divisions on the chart. Each chapter begins with an illustration and definition of the particular form of responsibility being dealt with. This opening illustration is like a case study, a typical, true-to-life situation that may seem familiar to you.

The illustration is followed by a list of methods from which parents can pick and choose—essentially, a menu of ways to teach that form of responsibility. The methods for younger children (starting with age four) are always first in the list, and those designed more for older children (to age twelve) are last.

Each chapter ends with some particularly effective practices that are called "family focal points." These can become consistent habits within a family to instill and preserve that form of responsibility within the children. The focal points are more personal, a specific idea or two from our own family that we think might help other families keep a particular form of responsibility "alive and well" over the months and years ahead. You will notice that the methods sections of each chapter is composed of games, songs, stories, and other activities that teach children a certain form of responsibility and that are used only when you are *concentrating* on teaching the kind of responsibility covered by that particular chapter. The "family focal points," on the other hand, are practices, patterns, or traditions that you may want to make permanent and habitual in your family.

To succeed in teaching responsibility to children and to make best use of the ideas in this book, it is crucial to acknowledge and understand six important principles.

1. *Every child is different.* Nothing is more evident to us as we raise our children than the fact that each one is unique and different from the others. Just as each one responds to discipline differently, so will each respond to responsibility differently. Although some things must be done uniformly, we should remember that different children require different kinds of motivation (for example, some need more *pushing,* others need more *sensitivity*).

2. *Expectations determine performance.* One amusing thing that we keep learning over and over about teaching responsibility is that children do exactly what is *really* expected of them. (And they can tell if you're faking it.)

One mother we know who had plenty of money to hire household help felt that her children, especially her girls, would be making beds and doing dishes for the rest of their lives once they were married. Since the family could afford it, she had decided that now was the time to let them spend their time with skiing, sewing, tennis, and piano lessons while a maid did the work around the house. You may agree or disagree with this philosophy, but the point is that those girls did what was expected of them as far as household responsibilities were concerned—exactly nothing.

3. *Example is the best teacher.* An important tool in teaching children responsibility of any kind is example. Children are much less likely to keep their rooms clean if the kitchen is always a disaster and the family room a jumbled mess. If father always leaves his socks wherever they drop, waits for mother to hang up his suit, and never seems to get to the leaky faucet and broken screens, the children will notice.

Once in a while we need to step back and look at ourselves. If we are trying to teach our children something we never learned, maybe our first step is to change ourselves.

Also, remember the connection between respect and responsibility. If you show respect for things, for work, for other people, then you see those things as important, and thus show responsibility for them. Your children, watching, will do likewise.

4. *Consistency is crucial.* Consistency and follow-through are, without a doubt, the hardest part of teaching responsibility. When we had our firstborn child, we looked into those baby eyes and daydreamed about a lovely ten-year-old who would come into our room dressed and ready for piano practice at 6:30 A.M. She would leave her room clean and tidy and eat a good breakfast before school, then on returning from school, go straight to her homework and afternoon responsibilities. If that little baby had realized what would be expected of her, she would have been amazed—but it would not have compared with the shock we would have undergone if we had realized what was required of *us* in order to make that dream come true.

It's easy and logical to say, "Now, Josh, go clean your room so that you can go to the store with us." But it is *not* easy when you realize that time is short and you've got to get to the store and back, prepare dinner, find a baby-sitter, and leave for the evening. It's even harder to leave him home when you find that his room is still a mess, knowing that his best friend is having a birthday party and he desperately wants to buy the present himself. But learn he must, and if you take him to the store before he cleans that room, the message is clear: "Mom doesn't really mean it."

We have to be pretty tough-skinned at times in order to be

consistent. The sooner we realize that the amount of responsibility our children learn depends on our consistency and our follow-through—no matter how difficult it may be—the better off we are. There is nothing more challenging in terms of patience, understanding, and courage.

5. *Children learn from what is really happening.* You may know, as we do, of some parents who are pretty good at manipulating their children. They manipulate them to be polite or to get A's in school.

And the children are always learning. The trouble is, they are not learning what the parents think they are teaching. They are learning to manipulate.

We have to teach principles and then give initiative and responsibility to our children. Most importantly, we must be genuine ourselves. Our prime concern must be for *their* welfare, *their* learning and well-being, not for our convenience or our reputation and image with others.

6. *Pride is the sustaining force behind responsibility.* Children become capable of accepting responsibility as they learn to feel the right kind of pride in themselves and in their maturity and individuality.

They internalize responsibility for work as they learn to take pride in the job they do, for things as they take pride in their belongings, for potential as they find pride in whom they are becoming, and so on. Often it is a parent's praise that leads to a child's pride.

By design, *Teaching Children Responsibility* is more a program-to-be-used than it is a book-to-be-read. Parents lead complex lives, with various interests and responsibilities tugging at them from all sides. Too often parenting is a low priority. We pay it lip service. We know, theoretically, how important it is, but we often do it by reaction, situation by situation, without any real strategy or plan.

Teaching Children Responsibility is a program that, when followed, brings measurable, noticeable, wonderful results. But it is not easy, and it cannot be done subconsciously. It's not merely a question, in other words, of whether you agree with the theories of the book, but a question of whether you take the time and make the effort to put the book *into practice* with your own children. In short, it is a question of whether you take the responsibility of teaching responsibility.

There are two ways to use the book. The first is simply to try to teach each of your children the kind of responsibility that is most appropriate to his or her own age (i.e., concentrate on responsibility for "obedience," "things," and "work" with your five-year-old and on responsibility for "choices" and "potential" with your ten-year-old). This approach is probably the simplest if you have only one or two children. On the other hand, if you have several, it will become rather complicated to try to concentrate, at the same time, on many different types of responsibility for many different children. Also, you may have a ten-year-old who has not yet grasped the responsibilities for "things" or for "work" and is thus not ready for the "graduate course" on "potential" or "character."

The other approach, and the one we believe usually works best, is to focus as a family on one separate responsibility (one chapter) each month. The book has twelve chapters, one for each month of the year. Each chapter has a range of methods for teaching that particular form of responsibility, and the methods are arranged according to how basic they are. Thus, in a given month you could concentrate on a particular type of responsibility, choosing the methods and practices most appropriate for the individual ages of your children.

In a month when you are concentrating on an "early" responsibility (such as responsibility for things), you might work hardest with your younger children, involving the older ones in teaching and in setting the example. In a month when you work on a more advanced responsibility (such as responsibility for contribution), you might concentrate principally on your older children and involve the younger ones with only the most basic methods and stories included in that chapter.

If you choose this approach, remember that your family's efforts should be cumulative. The major patterns you develop in April while working on the responsibility for actions should be well enough implanted that they continue to function somewhat automatically during May when you shift your conscious efforts to the responsibility for talents.

When you have followed the program for a full year, start over. The children are now a year older. They have a year's experience. They (and you) can now understand each particular form of responsibility more clearly and develop it more thoroughly.

One other caution: Don't become overwhelmed! There

are hundreds of methods in the book; no parent can use all of them all the time. In fact, no one can even think about or recall all of them all the time.

So don't try. Simplify by concentrating and focusing on one form of responsibility each month. You *can* keep one thing in mind and be aware of it consistently. In fact, as you focus on one, you will find yourself reinforcing it and implementing it subconsciously. You'll be surprised at how well you'll do.

Even as you concentrate on only one form of responsibility at a time, you may ask when we find time to tell the stories or have the discussions or play the games that are given as methods. Try dinner time. As families get older, they need one time to be together. Make it the dinner hour and turn that dinner hour into a discussion time, a teaching time, a learning time.

SECTION 1

RESPONSIBILITY TO PARENTS

The first subject children can learn to be responsible to is you, their parent.

In that context, it is quite easy to decide what you would like them to be responsible for. They should be responsible to you first for obedience because they are your children. Second, they should become responsible for the things they have received. Third, they should gain responsibility for portions of the family work because they are part of your family.

These three responsibilities—obedience, things, and work—are closely tied together, not only because they are all responsibilities to you, but because they feed and grow on each other. Much of a child's obedience relates to caring for his things and doing his work. A child learns to take care of his things through the experience of work and of obedience. And a child learns to be responsible for work largely in response to obedience and in pursuit of things.

The responsibilities of things and work are particularly closely associated because children cannot feel fully responsible for things until they feel as though they own them, and they rarely feel that they own them unless they have had to work for them.

Responsibility for Obedience 1

Obedience is the first step on the responsibility staircase. Without it, other forms of responsibility are hard to reach.

A. *Definition and Illustration*

The world we live in requires obedience—not conformity, not stereotype, but obedience to the laws of nature, the laws of society, the laws of morality and higher values. Obedience does not diminish freedom, it increases it. By teaching our children to obey, we open channels through which we can teach them everything else.

The objective of this chapter is to help our children see obedience as a desirable thing and as a route to happiness as well as to responsibility.

Lucy, a precocious five-year-old, had a particular quality that sometimes delighted her parents and sometimes infuriated them. When it delighted them, they called it "individuality," "a strong will," "uniqueness." When it infuriated them, they called it "stubbornness," "defiance," "cussedness."

In its second form, the quality included extreme and intense disobedience. When Lucy was told to come to dinner, she always had an excuse. When she was told to put away her toys, she procrastinated and found excuses and never quite got it done. When she was told to turn off the television and put on her pajamas, she often said, simply, "No."

To be sure, this irritated her parents, but Lucy's will was usually stronger than theirs. They had other things on their minds, and it was usually easier to drop the point than to force Lucy to mind. Occasionally, either because the disobedience became unbearably blatant or because other pressures had lowered the boiling point, father or mother would enforce a point, tell Lucy to do it or else, and usually end up spanking her when she chose the "or else."

Recently, as often happens with four- and five-year-olds, Lucy's favorite word had become "why?" She sometimes linked the word in a great chain of "whys" that tied her parents in knots. "Why do I have to eat those peas?" "Why will they make me grow big?" "Why does everyone have to get big?" "Why does the world work that way?"

Lucy's parents resorted to the answer that hog-tied parents have resorted to for generations: "Because I said so, that's why." Even that didn't stop Lucy. She said, "*Why* do you say so?" On another, particularly defiant day she said, "You'll have to come up with a better reason than that!"

Then, one day, Lucy's mother attended a parenting seminar in which the speaker emphasized three principles about laws: (1) Children should understand that family laws are sensible counsel from parents who love them, and that obeying rules minimizes hurt and maximizes happiness. (2) Children must learn that laws are absolutely consistent, that they will always apply and always be enforced. (3) Children must know that parents do not seek obedience to satisfy their own ego needs, but because they want their children to obtain rewards and avoid punishments.

That evening Lucy's parents had a long discussion about applying these principles. They all seemed applicable, appropriate, and needed. Could they, with Lucy's cooperation, develop some clear and simple family laws? Could Lucy be helped to understand the reasons for each law and to think in terms of obeying laws rather than obeying people? Could they apply the laws, along with their rewards and punishments, clearly and consistently? Could Lucy learn that the laws were a manifestation of her parents' love for her and that keeping the laws brought happiness?

Yes to each question! They took the time to gather as a family to explain to Lucy the general and the specific concepts involved, to let her give her ideas and vote on theirs.

Almost instantly, obedience took on a different meaning in the home—and in Lucy's mind. Instead of a contest of the will where the bigger people could win by force, obedience became simply a question of whether one wanted the positive or negative consequences, the rewards or the penalties. The same precociousness and strong will that had previously made Lucy so unmanageable now made her intrigued with the new concept of laws and determined to live them and prove them.

Under the new system, Lucy's life (not to mention that of her parents) became happier and simpler. The family laws were readjusted occasionally, always in conference with Lucy, to fit new circumstances.

There was, however, one remaining obedience problem in Lucy's home. Lucy had learned to respect and obey laws but still had problems obeying her parents in "non-law" situations. She did well on things like "get ready for bed now," because bedtime was a family law. She could tell time, and it was the clock that decided on when she should go to bed, not her parents. But problems still existed with such things as, "Lucy, you'd better wear your coat today, it's a little chilly," or "Turn the television off now; you've watched enough for one day." That sort of command was, to Lucy, a judgment call, and she was still very much in possession of her strong will. She even managed to turn the new family law structure to her side of the argument by saying, "Well, there's no law about *that!*"

Some areas of difficulty were overcome easily by the creation of new family laws. The family did, for example, agree on a policy regulating the amount of television to be seen each week, but to list too many laws diluted their importance, and there were always situations that would not fall under the jurisdiction of even a very long list.

The problem was solved (or at least a big step was taken toward its solution) one evening when Lucy's father was in a particularly good mood because of a recent business success. He asked Lucy to pick up some papers that the dog had pulled out of the wastebasket. Lucy gave him the "There's-no-law-about-that" routine. Instead of taking his usual "I-don't-care-if-there's-a-law-or-not-you-mind-your-father" stance, he sat down, cross-legged, on the floor with Lucy and did some explaining:

"Lucy, let me explain something to you. The way the world works is that people who have children teach them to be happy and to be good. Then these little people grow up and get married and have other children, and they teach *them* to be happy and to be good. Your mom and I are responsible for you. That means we teach you and care for you and love you until you are old enough to be on your own. When children don't learn to be obedient, they make mistakes and become unhappy. When you were born, Mommy and I promised each other that we would be responsible for you and take care of you. If we didn't love you, we might let you do anything you wanted, and not have any laws and not tell you the right things to do.

"Good mommies and daddies have the responsibility to know what's best for their children and to be sure they do it. And good children have the responsibility to obey their parents.

"I promise you that Mommy and I will try our hardest to make only good laws and to ask you to do only things we think are best. That is our responsibility. And your responsibility is to obey us. That way you'll learn obedience and be able to obey other kinds of laws too.

"Now, I think you should pick up those papers. Everyone in our family needs to help around the house, and I asked you to do that because it's good for you to help."

As time passed, Lucy's parents came to feel that there were two basic keys to Lucy's obedience. One key was to have a basic set of well-understood family laws so that in most situations she was obeying a law rather than a person. The second key was to have a clear understanding of parent responsibility and child obedience-responsibility to cover behavior that did not fall under one of the family laws.

In our own family, particularly with our first children, obedience never seemed quite obtainable. We worked hard at it, with methods ranging from militaristic "yes-sir" type obedience to more subtle efforts involving code words designed to remind children to do something without coming right out and telling them.

Following are some of the methods that work, not just in the mechanical sense of getting children to obey, but in the deeper sense of helping them understand *why* they should obey and in building a foundation of parental obedience on which to build the superstructure of responsibility in their lives.

B. Methods

1. *Story: "Cheekey and the Laws."* (This story, printed originally in the book *Teaching Children Joy,* is a good place to begin with small children.)

Cheekey was a monkey. He lived with his sister and his mother and father in a tree in the jungle. In the jungle there were some laws called Jungle Laws. Do you know what laws are? (Things that you must do right or else you get punishment.)

Do you know what a punishment is? (Something sad that happens when you break a law.)

There were two laws in the jungle. One was that whenever you were in a tree, you had to hold on with your hand, or your foot, or your tail. What do you think the punishment was if you broke that law? (You would fall!)

The other law was that if you saw a lion coming, you had to quickly climb up a tree. What do you think the punishment was if you broke that law? (You would get eaten!)

In Cheekey's own family tree, there were two family laws. One law was that you couldn't go out of the tree without asking. Why do you think they had that law? (So Cheekey wouldn't get lost.)

Why didn't his mother and father want him to get lost? (Because they loved him.)

What do you think the punishment was if Cheekey went out of his tree without asking? (His mother gave him a swat with her tail.)

Why did his mother do that? (So he wouldn't go out of the tree again.)

Why didn't she want him to do it again? (Because she loved him and didn't want him to get lost.)

The other monkey family law was to never drop banana peels on limbs of the family tree. Why do you think they had that law? (So no one would slip on them and fall out of the tree.)

Why did the monkey family decide to have a law like that? (Because they loved each other and didn't want anyone in their family to get hurt.)

What do you think the punishment was for breaking that law? (A swat.)

Why would the mother do that? (Because she loved Cheekey and wanted him to remember not to do it again.)

Sometimes there were laws to tell Cheekey what to do, and sometimes there weren't any laws and he could decide for himself.

When Cheekey first woke up in the morning, he had to stretch and yawn, and he almost let go of the branch. Was there a law to tell him what to do? (Yes—hold on or he would fall.)

Then he looked at his two hats, a red one and a green one. Was there a law to tell him which one to wear? (No—he could choose whichever one he wanted.) He chose the red one.

Then he wanted to climb down out of the tree to find a banana for breakfast. Was there a law to tell him what to do? (Yes—ask his mother so she would know where he was and so he wouldn't get lost.)

He found a big banana and a little banana. Was there a law to tell him which one to choose? (No—he could choose either one he wished.) Cheekey chose the big one because he was very hungry.

While he was walking back to his tree, he saw a lion. Was there a law to tell him what to do? (Yes—climb up a tree quickly or the lion would eat him!)

Cheekey climbed up a tree. After the lion went away, he went back to his own tree and wondered which limb to sit on to eat the banana. Was there a law to tell him where to sit? (No—he could choose any limb he wanted.)

When he peeled the banana, was there a law about the peel? (Yes—don't leave it on a limb.)

Cheekey had an enjoyable, safe day. It's fun and safe when you know the laws and do what they say, and it's fun to decide things when there isn't a law about them.

2. *Comparison story: The Smiths and the Joneses.* (To help *small* children want to have family laws and want to live them.

Draw (or let the children draw) on a blackboard or large sheet of paper two houses, similar in size, next door to each other. Using the drawing as a visual aid, tell the following story in your own words:

"In this house (*point to one of the houses*) lived the Smith family. They had a boy and a girl named Steve and Sue. And they had *no* family laws. They didn't have to come to dinner at any certain time or go to bed at any certain time. They didn't have to put away their toys; they didn't have to mind their mother and father; they could watch television any time they wanted. In fact, their parents let them do just about anything they wanted. (*Point to the other house.*) In this house lived the Jones family. They had a boy named Jimmy and a girl named Janie. They had family laws, and the children knew that they would be punished if they broke the laws.

"Now let's pretend we can see right inside each of these houses and watch what is happening. Let's look into the Smith house first. Look at Steve and Sue's rooms. They look like pigpens. Nothing is put away; everything is on the floor. But where are Steve and Sue? Oh, there's Sue watching television. Her homework's not done. She'll be sorry tomorrow when her teacher asks her a question and she doesn't know the answer. There's Steve across the fence playing with a friend. His mom called him for dinner, but he didn't come. Now his food is cold and soggy. Look, his face is scratched from a fight with Sue over a toy. They don't even have laws against fighting.

"Let's look inside the Jones house. Jimmy's and Janie's clothes and toys are all neat and tidy, because their family has a law about that. Their family members are all sitting together having a nice dinner because they have a law about that. Jimmy and Janie did their homework before dinner because they have a law for that, too. When they've finished eating, they will be able to play and not worry about school tomorrow."

Make your story personal by including things that are relevant to your family. Then involve the children in a discussion based on the following questions: Are laws good or bad? Do they make us happy or sad? Would we like to be like the Smiths? Should grown-ups have to obey laws too? What are some of our national laws? What are some of our community laws? What are some of our family laws? How does each make us happy?

3. *Family meeting.* (To formalize family laws that children help create and thus feel responsible for keeping.)

Sit down together with a blank chart and marking pens and hold a family meeting to create (or formalize) your family laws.

Indicate that anyone can propose a law, but that it won't be put on the chart until it is discussed and voted for unanimously by the family.

Steer the discussion in such a way that the laws are simple and direct. Don't end up with too many. Arrive together at an appropriate "punishment" for the breaking of each law. Use natural consequences or a close approximation of them for punishments wherever possible. For example, the punishment for not coming on time to dinner could be no dinner. The punishment for not cleaning one's room could be staying in the room until it is clean. The punishment for yelling or screaming could be going in one's room where others don't have to listen. If spanking is to be a punishment, it should be done only with the hand, and should be used only for serious violations that hurt others.

Write the agreed-on punishment beside the law to which it applies. Vote on the punishment as well as the laws. Discuss each until everyone is in agreement.

Keep the laws visible. Enforce them consistently. Alter them as needed, but only through further family meetings.

4. *Family meeting to make mutual commitments.* (To make parent directives more thoughtful and child obedience more predictable.)

Gather the family together, and tell the children that you want them to know of some commitments that you (as parents) have made. Explain that you not only love each of the children more than anything else, but that you feel that they are your greatest responsibility and the most important thing in your lives.

Tell them that you want to make them a promise and to ask them to make a promise to you in return. Your promise is that you will do your best to be wise parents, to help them to be wise, and to always say and do the things that you feel are best for them. Tell them that you won't give them everything they want or let them do everything they want, because that would not be wise, and because you love them too much to give up your responsibility for them.

As you make these serious promises, look each child in the eye, and speak to him on his own level.

Then ask them for a promise in return—a promise of obedience, a promise that they will obey you and obey the family laws. Ask that their promise be as serious and sincere as yours.

Do anything you can to make the moment memorable and the promises lasting. You may wish to conclude by raising your hands together and making a "joint pledge."

5. *Role reversal.* (To help children see things from your perspective, and you from theirs.)

When a serious disagreement arises concerning obedience in a particular matter, sit back for a moment, let things calm down, and then ask the child to pretend he's the mommy or daddy and you are the child. Set the stage for him. Tell him *why* he wants you, the child, to do (or not do) the particular thing. Then start the game.

Be a convincing "child." Play the role well and make your "parent" explain to you why he wants you to obey.

Some children role-play more naturally than others, but all children can learn the technique, and often it can be very helpful.

6. *Apologizing.* (To give children a chance to "put things right" and to teach them that punishment can sometimes be avoided by a sincere apology.)

When a child breaks a law and you sense that he's truly sorry he has done so, tell him he has a choice: to accept the punishment that goes with the law he has broken, or to apologize. Apologizing, for a small child, should involve asking forgiveness from the person he has hurt or offended and promising not to do it again.

Apologizing is particularly appropriate when one child has hurt another. If the child will hug the one he has hurt, ask his forgiveness, and promise not to hurt him again, he should be able to avoid the punishment (as long as he has not committed the same offense recently). This will often do more toward restoring good feelings than any punishment would.

C. Family Focal Points: Family Laws and "Trigger Words"

Many years ago, when our oldest daughters were four and three, we created our first "Family Law Chart." We had talked of laws as things that make a home orderly and happy. Now we sat down to let the children help us formulate our set of laws. We told them that laws were to tell us the things we must do and the things we must not do.

To our amazement, they understood! Saren's hand went up and our first law was proposed: "Don't ruin things that aren't for ruining!" We all voted yes on that one. She had another one: "Don't hit other little girls." Another unanimous vote. Then Shawni got into the act. She remembered a scolding she had received earlier that day for playing with an electrical plug and outlet. "Don't pud in puds." We went on until we had sixteen laws—too many, but certainly better than none.

Not long afterward, we discussed and listed punishments—a specific one for each law. Still later, Saren approached me and said, "Dad, our laws are too complicated, and there are too many of them. The little kids can't even remember them all." That led to a simplification process. If all of Israel was governed by ten commandments, we ought to be able to handle our little family with five.

We ended up with five one-word laws:

1. Peace
2. Order
3. Asking
4. Obedience
5. "Pegs"

"Peace" includes things ranging from the original "Don't hit other little girls" to avoiding loud words, anger, or screaming. "Order" covers leaving rooms in order, taking out only one toy at a time, and putting away anything you use. "Asking" means never going somewhere, or using something of someone else's, without asking. "Obedience" means minding Mother and Father (more on that in a moment). And "Pegs" means getting the pegs (which represent family jobs and procedures) in our family pegboard each day (discussed in detail in chapter 3).

Punishments for violations of each law are clearly defined and appear on the law chart.

We found that once the laws were simplified and clearly connected to their punishments, the principle of apologizing began to work. The children realized that if they were genuinely sorry for breaking a law, we would allow them to avoid its punishment by asking forgiveness from whomever they had hurt or offended and by promising to try hard not to do it again.

Much of the disobedience that occurs in families is often simply a bad habit. Children give excuses, whine, and say "That's not fair" largely out of a pattern that they get into. We made some progress in breaking that habit through using simple "trigger words."

We held a family meeting in which we pledged our care and best efforts to the children while they pledged obedience to us. Then we decided that we needed a signal that would indicate to the children: "We've thought about what we're asking you to do. We think it is best, and you should obey." They, in turn, needed a simple signal or trigger word to show us that they understood. They needed a "habit word" that prompted the good habit of obedience.

We picked the simplest words: *please* from us, and *yes, Mommy* or *yes, Daddy* from them. If Richard says, "Josh, time to put that away and get ready for bed" and he starts to say, "Oh, but Daddy, can't I just—" Richard says, "Please," which is his trigger to say, "Yes, Daddy," and do it.

The strongly emphasized *please* needs to be used carefully. Sometimes it may be well to let Josh do "just one more thing." But the point is, when the parent says "please" (or whatever other trigger word is decided on), the child knows it is a clear request and is obligated to say "Yes, Daddy" and do it instantly.

In our family, the law chart provides the focal point for law-obedience, and the trigger words provide the focal point for parent-obedience. Together they can help even very small children learn this first aspect of responsibility.

Remember that laws and obedience are not only the first rung of the responsibility ladder, but they are also tremendous sources of security to children. A home that is ordered and based on clear procedures and rules of conduct, a home where authority is clearly defined, a home with consistency and discipline—such a home is the most secure and most confidence-breeding environment in which a child's life can take shape.

However, please don't assume, after you sit down as a family and carefully draw up the family laws and punishments, that somehow your children will turn into lovely, obedient angels overnight. The principles involved are good, and they work, but not without much ado. We have had at least twenty-five family meetings in which we have discussed family laws. After every violation, we talk about them. We have defended our purpose in using them and enforcing them. The children have talked about them with each other, and we have somehow managed to drag them with us through the complaints and hard times. Obedience in children does not develop overnight, especially when the children are not used to the idea of following laws or of being obedient. It is just not easy!

It is a valuable exercise to sit down as parents and think about the obedience level in your own family. It is easy for us to get so used to certain responses from our children that we don't even realize that they're not being obedient.

Several years ago when we were living in England, Joyce, an outspoken young English girl who was helping Linda one day, couldn't help hearing a conversation between Linda and our oldest daughter, Saren (who was six). It was quite a heated conversation. After it was over and Saren disappeared, Joyce said, "Why do you let Saren talk to you like that?"

"Like what?" Linda asked, amazed that she would think it was peculiar.

"Like she did this afternoon when you were 'having words' with her. Americans seem to let their children speak to them in such a dreadful manner!"

Linda was shocked, but she has come to be grateful to Joyce for that question, because it might otherwise have taken her quite some time to recognize that Saren really did have a nasty tone in her voice when she disagreed with her. She had been speaking with near contempt. Linda simply had tuned out the offensiveness in her voice because she'd heard it often. But in thinking about it, she decided that Joyce was absolutely right and that things were going to change!

"It's all right to ask questions," Linda told Saren that evening, "but you must remember to use a respectful tone of voice."

Occasionally she ventures too near the line, but when we give her a certain signal, she remembers and calms down.

The same principle applies to obedience. We parents get so used to giving orders that we don't really expect to be carried out that the children's ears become deaf and our minds become numb to the facts. Children will do exactly what their parents expect. They are very perceptive, and they do know exactly what is expected of them. A soul-searching family conference on the subject is highly recommended. It may change lots of bad habits that you hardly realized were there.

It is also important to remember that even though children know they should be obedient and are trying, some try harder than others. We have one particular child who occasionally has a more difficult time than the others in being obedient. We realize, even as we write, that instructions have been going in one ear and out the other for several days. She has to be asked to do her jobs several times and still may not finish them. It's time for a private consultation with this child to review the laws, talk about minding, and recommit her to the principle of her obedience. A one-on-one discussion often helps to correct things, but it still takes consistent follow-through and special emphasis to make her feel good about her obedience again.

The point is that teaching obedience is not easy and involves much more than just one or two easy lessons. So don't be discouraged. Persevere! It will make you happy, and most important, it will make your children happy. In spite of all they say, they love to obey!

Responsibility for Things 2

It is unlikely that a child will accept responsibilities that he cannot see, such as talents, potential, jobs, or character, until he accepts responsibilities he can see—his possessions.

A. Definition and Illustration

Most of us have too many material possessions. As our society becomes more complex and our lives have more and more facets, "things" can begin to overtake us. More than ever before, in order to live happily, it is necessary to simplify, organize, and be responsible for things. The goal of this chapter is to offer some precise suggestions to parents about how to get children to feel and accept this responsibility and to learn to control things before things begin to control them!

George and Nancy Cuthbert were meticulous people. Some would have called them perfectionists. Everything had a place, and everything was in that place. Disorderliness drove them crazy. Perhaps the fact that they were both that way is what attracted them to each other in the first place.

They had been married for nearly ten years and had three children. Their oldest child, Jimmy, was proof of the heredity factor. He was as neat and tidy as they were. His room looked as though it were ready to be photographed for a better-homemaking article.

But the next two children, Ginny, eight, and Phillip, six, were another story. No amount of coaxing, bribing, punishing, or encouraging could persuade them to take care of their things. Their rooms looked as if they had been hit by a hurricane. Though Nancy cleaned their rooms often, five minutes later they once again looked as if a hurricane had struck.

Finally, Nancy had had it. She decided that if they wanted to live in filth and disarray, it was just too bad. She determined never to look in their rooms at all. When she found one of their toys or an article of clothing scattered elsewhere in the house (a frequent occurrence), she marched to the door of the offender's room, turned her head the other way, opened the door, threw the article in, then quickly slammed the door shut again.

Ginny and Phillip didn't seem to notice. The only perceptible changes in them were that they looked a little more rumpled each day and they asked Nancy more often where things were.

"In your room," she always said.

"But *where* in our room?" they always said.

"I don't know. I haven't been in there for days," she always said.

"Why not?" they always asked.

"Because I don't like to go in messy places," she always said. Then they usually walked away, looking a bit confused.

It wasn't a technique. Nancy had given up on all the techniques. This was just her way of giving up altogether on the whole idea of making them responsible.

One day Ginny came into the kitchen and said, "Mom, where is that red blouse I like?"

Nancy said, "In your room," and the conversation followed its standard pattern.

Finally, Ginny said, "Well, it's gone, so you'll have to buy me another one."

"Not so," said Nancy. "When you own a thing and lose it, it's gone."

"Well, it's not really mine," said Ginny. "You bought it."

Nancy thought about that for a while. That afternoon she went to visit her sister's family. They had just returned from a year-long assignment in another city and had returned to their house only to discover how poorly the renters had cared for it. "People just don't take care of things unless they own them," her sister said.

Nancy made the connection in her mind. Ginny and Phillip somehow didn't perceive their things as *theirs*. They hadn't worked for them, and therefore they didn't value them.

But ownership wasn't the only reason for neatness, orderliness, and care, was it? After all, Jimmy had always taken care of his things, even when he was small, just for the pleasure and convenience of having things where they belonged.

During the next few days, while Nancy and George were trying to think of a way to help Ginny and Phillip feel the responsibility of ownership, the children's constantly messy rooms began to have an effect. Nancy had taken a couple of peeks in, and the levels of rubbish were now nearly knee-deep. She also noticed one day that Phillip had tried to pick up a few things to make a path in his room.

Then came an unexpected breakthrough. Ginny came downstairs one day and said, "Mom, will you help me clean up my room, please?"

"Whatever for?" said Nancy.

"I'm just getting sick of it like that," said Ginny, "and besides, I can't find anything."

Nancy acted on her first impulse. "Does Phillip feel the same way?"

"I think so," replied Ginny.

"Then get him down here, and let's make a deal."

When they were both sitting in front of her, Nancy said, "Okay, here's the deal. I'll help each of you clean your room this one time, but they are *your* rooms, and from now on it's *your* responsibility to keep your things put away. From now on, whenever I see anything left out or in the wrong place, I won't put it away, and I won't throw it on the floor of your room either. What I will do is put it on your bed. Then every night before bedtime you have to take the things off your bed and put them away. Is it a deal?"

The children agreed. There were some regressions now and then, but basically the plan worked. They soon found that a bed full of toys and clothes was a very unpleasant thing to confront at night when they were tired, so they gradually left less and less out of place.

Nancy and George realized that not all children are the same. Some, like Jimmy, are motivated to take care of things out of their simple attraction to neatness. Others take care of things only when there are practical, *ownership* reasons for doing so. George and Nancy eventually found a way to give their children a stronger sense of ownership to supplement the "things-on-the-bed" method. They developed a system of paying Ginny and Phillip for some general household jobs and arranged other ways of helping them earn their own money, which they used to buy their own toys and clothes. Over time, this approach worked even better than the "things-on-the-bed" because it provided an actual fact of worked-for ownership. Where the "bed" method had been merely a technique, the ownership method was more of a principle; it worked on the basis of pride and of genuine care for one's own things. (This "ownership" method is explained in more detail in the "family focal point" of this chapter.)

Linda says this:

The more we analyze teaching the responsibility for material things, the more we realize, once again, that the key to success is remembering the never-ending quest to improve *ourselves.*

I have a confession to make. I am not a Nancy or a George. I am not a naturally tidy person. I somehow managed to blunder through high school and college, excusing my disastrous room with obligations to practice and leadership responsibilities at school. My dad used to jokingly call me "Mrs. Smith," the name of a particularly disorganized neighbor. (One day I asked to use her phone, and after picking my way through the debris to the phone, I turned around to see their dead Christmas tree still decorated in the corner. It was March.)

At college I had a roommate who was as untidy as I, and though we both did well in school and were gone most of the time studying or practicing, we always returned to a room that looked very much as though someone had thrown a hand grenade in and shut the door. Occasionally I'd turn over a new leaf, but it was short-lived.

It seems to me that I improved for a while after our marriage, thinking how embarrassed I'd be if *he* found out how bad I was. As children came along, however, things began to get muddled again, and I began getting up in the morning to a sink full of dirty dishes that I had just been too tired to wash the night before.

After four children and many, many commitments to try harder, I finally reached the point where I could no longer tolerate the messy rooms at night, the lost shoes, clothes, scissors, papers, and so forth. We decided in earnest that the time had arrived. All the "wouldn't it be nice" ideas were to be implemented. I quickly realized that any plan had to start with me, the mother!

A good friend taught me the principle of touching things only once, which helped immensely. For example, if your recipe calls for salt, take it from the cupboard, put it in the mix, and return it to the cupboard all in one movement. When washing clothes, put the item straight from the dryer into a basket labeled for the appropriate person. The list goes on and on, but as I implemented the principle, I found that the clutter began to disappear.

All in all, I can honestly say that since I have started putting away all my own things, have seen that my own bed was the first one made, and have followed through with the children's responsibility for their things, our home has been a different place. I would not have believed that it could make so much difference!

Again, it is not easy. This has been one of the hardest aspects of parenting for me, maybe because I was so bad at it. But the reward is certainly worth the effort.

B. Methods

1. *Family laws.* (To help children see that orderliness and care of one's things is an expected and mandatory part of membership in the family.)

As discussed earlier, simple, clear, high-awareness-level family laws are the most basic way to establish behavior patterns. One law should deal with the care and orderliness of each person's things. The punishment connected with violation of this law should tie directly to the problem itself. A child should have to stay in his room until it's clean—he eats no dinner until it is. Or, if Nancy's "things-on-the-bed" method is used, he should have to put each thing in its place before his bedtime. The idea is to show the very real inconvenience and unpleasantness of not caring for one's things.

As with all family laws, the keys to effectiveness are simple but not easy. There are two that are especially important: First, be sure the law is understood. Children must participate in and vote on its creation and must know exactly what is required and precisely what the punishment is for breaking it. Second, be consistent. Laws that are enforced erratically not only do little or no good, they actually can do harm by teaching children that laws are made to be broken.

2. *Example.* (To show children that being responsible for one's things is a source of satisfaction and joy, and to be sure that they know how to care for their things.)

Bring your children in to watch as you put away your own things, as you shine your shoes, as you put away your own kitchen utensils. Let them see that you have a place for each thing. Let them watch you wash the car or oil the lawn mower or polish the silver. Let them see the pride you feel in caring for your things. Don't lecture them or make the connections to them too obvious. Instead of saying, "See how well I take care of my things? You should take good care of your things too," say, "I really like to take care of my things; it makes me feel happy inside," or "It's fun to have a place for everything and put everything in its right place. I feel good when everything is neat and clean."

3. *Ownership tags.* (To help children realize that certain things are theirs, and that they are responsible for them.)

Small, round, self-stick tags with the child's name on them can go a long way toward helping each child to put toys and other belongings away. Particularly in the early years, when children have just learned to write their names, those names are a source of pride and identity to them. Seeing their names on articles not only helps to establish the ideas of ownership and responsibility, it also creates a desire to "care for" and to "take pride in."

4. *"In-place" tags or outlines.* (To help children connect a certain thing with a certain place.)

We've all seen the mechanic's workroom or the woodworker's tool wall on which the shadow outline of a tool or wrench is painted on the surface where the tool hangs or the shelf where it sits. A similar system can help children get it into their minds that their own things each have a particular place.

A variation of this idea also works with clothes. One drawer can be labeled *socks* (either with a picture or the word), a certain shelf labeled *shoes,* and so forth.

5. *Simplification.* (To make the whole concept of responsibility for things simpler by simply having fewer things.)

While it may not be a method, this is perhaps the most effective of all ways to teach children to be responsible for their things. In many families there are simply too many things. Children have too many toys, too many clothes, too much to keep track of.

We learned this lesson graphically when we began spending our summers at a small lakeside cabin in Idaho. Because the cabin is small, the children are allowed to bring only a couple of toys each. Because it is a lake and because it is summer, they take only a swimming suit, one set of dressy clothes, and two sets of play clothes. It is heavenly! Nothing is out of place, because there are so few things.

The key in everyday situations is to simplify and to aim for quality rather than for quantity. Give a child one long-lasting, high-quality birthday present that he will care for and treasure rather than a dozen cheap things with planned obsolescence that, at worst, break or tear or become unusable in a week or, at best, hold his interest only briefly and then become part of the clutter.

The starting point is to clear everything out, get rid of all the low-quality, high-quantity junk—and of some nice things, too, if they are not often used and if they are poorly cared for. Give them to someone who will value them.

One effective way to rid yourself of superfluous things is the "Gunny Bag" method discussed in the family focal point section of this chapter.

6. *"Pride" sign.* (To help children discover a feeling of pride in their own neatness and care of things.)

On one rainy Saturday, I took three of our children (the messiest three, ages four, six, and eight) into my den and let them watch me clean it. I tried to express the satisfaction I felt from having things in place and cared for. They were moderately interested.

When I finished, I taped a large, brightly colored sign on the den door that said PRIDE. I didn't say anything about it, but, of course, they asked.

"*Pride* means that I'm proud of how my den looks," I said, "It means that I feel good because all my things are clean and neat."

"Can I get one of those on my door?" the six-year-old predictably asked first, and the other two chimed in.

"Yes, but first your rooms will have to be as neat as my den."

It worked. It still works. The signs go up periodically, whenever we need a booster on basic neatness.

It's not the sign that is important; it's the discussion and reinforcement built around it. Talk about how good neatness feels. Talk about how lucky we are to have certain things; talk about how much some people would like to have those things and how well they would take care of them if they did have them.

7. *Game—"Search and Rescue."* (To demonstrate to children that when things are not in their place we can waste a lot of time looking for them.)

Divide family members into teams, depending on the ages of your children. If they are old enough, each person can be a team by himself. If there are young children unable to do this activity on their own, pair them off with the older children.

Give each team an equal number of Search and Rescue cards face down. These cards can be made by drawing on three-by-five-inch index cards simple pictures of common household objects. Some objects that might be included are: paintbrush, crayon, comb, hammer, hairbrush, nails, ball, spoon, needle, safety pin, broom, thimble, hat, thread, and glasses. The more cards you use the longer the game will last, especially if your house is fairly cluttered.

When you say "go" they are to turn over the first card. Then they are to find that item in the house and bring it back to their rescue pile. All team members must go to find each item, and they may look for only one item at a time.

When they return an item to the rescue pile, they may turn over another card and rescue that item. When they have rescued all of their items they yell, "Rescued!" You then make note on the record sheet of the time it took to find all of their items. (If your home is a normal home, many of these items will be hard to find, as they will not be where they are normally kept.)

Reinforce this principle with your family: Things out of place slow us down and cause confusion all day long.

A few days later, play this game again and record a second set of times. After you have simplified, eliminated, and put your house in order, things will probably be easier to find and the times should look better.

Note: If you were one of the lucky families that had everything in place so that you completed the game smoothly and easily, comment on what an added benefit this is to your family. It gives you a head start on having an orderly home.

8. *Their goal.* (To help children feel that their effort to take responsibility for things is their idea as well as yours, and that it pleases them as well as you when they do well.)

One of the key methods referred to repeatedly in this book is the weekly goal-setting session (described in detail in chapter 9.)

Once you feel that a child has a basic grasp of the benefits of caring for his things, encourage him to make it one of his weekly goals to do this. A small child might have the goal of making his bed each day for a week without being asked or reminded. An older child might have a goal of reorganizing his room and establishing an exact place for everything.

When it is their own objective, children will move toward real assumption of responsibility for things. Until it becomes their goal, they are not really accepting responsibility.

C. Family Focal Points: "Gunny Bag," "Bed Throw," "Own Money," and "Physical Reorganization"

Richard says this: One day, several years ago, I came home to find a terrific mess in the downstairs playroom and children's bedrooms. It was one of those particularly irritating messes of clutter: small, cheap toys and various bits and pieces that none of the children really claimed as theirs but that seemed to get kicked around the house constantly.

I took a deep breath, ready to call for the children to "get down here and straighten up this pigpen," but before the words came out, I had a different idea. After all, I'd yelled those words before, and there had certainly been no lasting effect.

Instead, I found a large old cloth laundry bag and painted on it two large "monster" eyes and a nose, positioned so that the bag's drawstring opening was a mouth. Then I started making monster noises and dragging the bag around the house, putting any scattered or out-of-place articles into it.

It took only a couple of minutes to attract a full child audience, more amused than worried at this point, shouting, "What are you doing?" and "Who is that?"

"This is Gunny Bag," I said. "He lives in the attic, and every once in a while, without warning, he comes down here and gobbles up all the toys or clothes that are left lying around out of place." I tried to sound matter-of-fact and went right on "eating" the toys.

The children watched at first, then started asking questions like, "Can we get the things back?"

The answer was "Yes, on Saturday he spits them all up in a big pile, and if they are put right away, he doesn't eat them again. If they are left out, though, he gobbles them right up, and once he has eaten anything for the second time, he never spits it up again!"

Their eyes were wider now, and there was an occasional "Oh no, not that, Daddy." "It's not me eating them," I reminded them. "It's Gunny Bag."

In a few more moments they gave up talking and began scurrying about, trying to rescue their best things. But the Gunny Bag "ate" quite a lot, and the children got the message.

Since then, Gunny Bag has returned often. He is always unannounced, always a surprise. When he finds nothing out of place "to eat" in a given room, he cries miserably, much to the delight of the child who has thwarted him through his neatness.

Over time, Gunny Bag has accomplished two very worthwhile things for our family. First, he engenders the need to always keep things neat and tidy, since no one ever knows when he will descend from his lair in the attic. Second, he is like a good garden snake who eats up all the destructive insects. He gobbles up the little, unnecessary toys and objects that clutter a house, and once he has eaten something twice, it never comes back (it goes, in fact, to the welfare store). Thus Gunny Bag weeds out the unnecessary things and causes the necessary and valuable things to be kept securely in their places.

Tell the children that old Gunny Bag wants to have a contest or a bet with them. During the next two weeks you will be working on responsibility for things. Here is Gunny Bag's deal: If he finds twenty-five things (or more) to eat (toys out of place) during the next two weeks, the children have to give him one toy to eat and never give back! But if he eats less than fifteen things, then *he* (Gunny Bag) has to take the whole family to the drive-in for dinner.

In addition to Gunny Bag, we like to use the "things-on-the-bed" method that Nancy and George discovered (see the beginning of this chapter). Children actually see the things they've left out accumulating in one concentrated spot, and thus become more conscious of those things and more aware of the inconvenience they cause their parents and themselves by leaving them out.

One key thing that children must sooner or later learn responsibility for is money. We have decided that sooner is much better than later because accepting responsibility for money is the key to being responsible about other things.

About the time our oldest daughter turned eight, we

realized that we were not comfortable with the money situation between us and her. An allowance seemed so normal, yet we felt we were teaching the wrong principle by giving something for nothing. We had had many friends whose parents had given them money all their lives. Some could handle that until they were old enough to find a better substitute. Others seemed to rely on the dole forever. We saw roommates in college whose lives were controlled by how much their fathers sent them in a particular month. Others were totally irresponsible with the money they were given, their habits probably indicative of the attitude "It isn't mine anyway."

During the same time period, we were having trouble getting our two oldest girls to pick up their clothes and to practice their music without being nagged or artificially rewarded. We had tried everything from self-stick stars on charts to lollipops. Suddenly one day we thought of a solution—the same method Linda's mother had used with her.

Recognizing that it is hard (though not impossible) for an eight-year-old to earn money in the outside world, we decided to kill two birds with one stone and pay our daughter for practicing. Now before you label that "absurd bribery," let us explain.

We began by offering a small amount for each half hour of practice. Two half-hour sessions were expected each day, one on violin and one on piano. Next we proclaimed that if all the practicing had been completed at the end of the week (one hour each day), our daughter's money would be doubled. We calculated it so that it would take a month or so to save enough for a dress or a pair of shoes. In some cases we allowed an IOU to be written if just the right dress was found but funds were not yet earned.

It worked like a dream. As if by magic, her lovely new clothes were hung in the closet instead of left on the floor, because now they were really hers. Since then, we have had no trouble getting our oldest daughter to practice.

The second child has followed suit. She also earns money by practicing, but in her case there is even more interest in making money by baby-sitting for us. By the time she was nine she was probably one of the world's best baby-sitters. We paid her very low wages to start with, knowing that her need for money would increase with age, and so that she could feel that her raises are due to experience and excellent work.

By the time our oldest son was seven, he was a real entrepreneur. Although he is not as interested in clothes as the girls, he's fascinated with calculators and chemistry sets. He is not practicing music on a regular basis yet, but he is very much interested in Saturday jobs! (We also pay the children for individual Saturday jobs not included in their regular responsibilities.) On Saturday mornings he hounds us about what he can do to earn some money for something he's seen at the store. He also plans to raise potatoes and sell them door-to-door or from a stand on the corner.

Our children know they are on their own financially at age eight. (We make exceptions of special things on birthdays and Christmas, and for underclothes and socks, items they are less inclined to buy for themselves.)

Many creative ideas are generated when children want to earn their own money. Some children have natural good sense about money, and others have to learn by experience. Our premise, however, is that the time for children to learn these valuable lessons about money is when they are from eight to twelve years old. These lessons will greatly influence their happiness and freedom later in life.

During ages eight to twelve while the children do earn their own money and buy their own things, it is usually *us* that they earn it from. When they turn twelve, however, they are expected to earn it elsewhere—from paper routes, babysitting, and other out-of-the-home sources.

It is not only the earning of money but the handling of money that constitutes the beginning of fiscal responsibility. We have a "family bank" consisting of a large wooden chest with a combination lock on it. Each child (even the smaller ones who don't yet have "financial responsibility" but who do earn money for small jobs and errands) has a checkbook in which deposits and withdrawals are recorded. They can write checks only to us. The family bank pays exorbitant interest (10 percent every quarter—10 percent because the children can compute it easily). Children get a small "treat" out of the chest each time they make a deposit. The combined incentives of interest and a treat have made real savers out of our children—that and the fact that they quickly discover how soon their money is spent and gone if they don't put it into the bank.

Some families with small children, particularly those with many small children, may find that they need an even more drastic and dramatic method of keeping *things* in order. At the risk of having you think we have gone too far, let us share the "order system" that has evolved in our family.

At one point, with five children under eight, we admitted to ourselves that even with "Gunny Bag" and "bed throw" too many things were simply out of place—too much clutter, particularly in the children's rooms.

It occurred to us one day that the ultimate solution to messy rooms was to permanently remove from those rooms the things that contributed to the mess. We were ready to do some minor remodeling on our home anyway, so we decided to take a rather dramatic step.

We removed everything from the small children's rooms except their beds, their comforter quilts, and one small "treasure chest" box for each in which they could keep their most special and personal things. All toys were removed and put in a toy closet, and all clothes were removed to the expanded and enlarged "nerve center" laundry room. Racks were installed there for clothes on hangers, and all children's dressers were moved there. Three dirty clothes bins were built in next to the washer, one each for whites, dark colors, and light colors.

Then the small children were taught that their clothes could not go outside of the "nerve center" unless they were on their bodies. Likewise, toys could be removed from the toy closet only one at a time. Both the nerve center and the toy closet began to work a little like libraries, with children "checking out" things one at a time.

We still struggle, of course, to keep the nerve center and toy closet neat, but if there is disorderliness, at least it is more confined to those two places. As children grow older and prove themselves able to care for their things and keep them in order, they have the privilege of moving their dressers and clothes and their toys back into their own rooms.

We have also supplemented the program with a small chart in the nerve center on which children can write down any article of clothing or toy that was left out by someone else which *they* put away. The person who left a listed item out owes a dime to the person who put it away. The children readily accepted the fact that it is only fair to have to pay someone who puts away one of their things.

Responsibility for Work 3

"All work and no play" may make Jack a dull boy, but it doesn't happen very often today. The more frequent occurrence is "all play and no work"—and that makes Jack an irresponsible boy!

A. Definition and Illustration

Much of the satisfaction and joy of life comes from the acceptance and conscientious completion of work. Children who never learn to work not only fail to accomplish worthwhile things as adults, but they also forfeit one of the basic joys and fulfillments of life. In this chapter, we will explore ways that the responsibility of work can be simplified and given to children. We will also look at ways that the family work load can be shared so that it becomes drudgery to none and joy to all.

Craig and SueAnn Peterson woke up late. It was Saturday morning. From the family room they heard the pops and bangs and laughter of the television cartoons. It was a pleasant way to wake up—pleasant except for what they had to face next: getting the children to do their weekly jobs.

They both felt that it was necessary and important for their three children to feel part of the responsibility for the house, for doing their share, for learning the basics of how to work.

It surely was unpleasant, though. SueAnn thought about it while lying in bed. First, the children would argue about who got the easiest job. Then they would dillydally around, get distracted, lose the broom, and generally do everything in their power to wiggle out of, postpone, or half-finish the jobs.

Ten-year-old Allison, who should be setting the example, was the worst of all. The other two heard her complaining and followed suit. Allison was a bright, independent, and stubborn child, and she was capable of marshalling a long list of fairly credible reasons why she didn't want to, or couldn't, or shouldn't do her jobs.

"Actually, Mom, those are *your* jobs. Dad goes to work, we go to school, and you take care of the house. You don't have to go to work for Dad or go to school for me, so why should I have to clean the house for you?"

SueAnn literally bit her tongue—to keep from biting Allison. She realized that there was a message in what Allison was saying, a message *about Allison.* Her daughter did not understand the shared responsibility of a family. She saw the jobs as arbitrary assignments from the only person she viewed as responsible for those jobs.

That night the Petersons had a serious family meeting. The conclusions reached were simple and direct. Even Justin, their six-year-old, understood them.

1. We are all responsible for the house because we all live here and are part of a family.

2. Mom takes the biggest share of the burden because of Dad's job and the children's school, but we all help.

3. We'll have a family meeting at the first of each month and decide together who should do which jobs. Once we have agreed, we'll be sure we know *how* and *when* to do our jobs, and we won't complain about them all month.

Things improved for the Petersons, but they still needed several of this chapter's principles.

Linda recalls this:

One morning I awoke to the sound of urgent voices and the clatter of pans. We had all spent the night at my mother's house. I was roused from a deep sleep to hear Mom say in a rather urgent voice, "Shawni, don't just sit there—get this sweater on and come out and help us, quick!"

What on earth could be wrong? By the time I had pulled on my clothes and got to the kitchen, I could see that Mom had rousted three of the older children (ages nine, seven, and six) as well as their father out of bed at 6:00 A.M., and they were frantically picking beans in the garden.

I had been cold in the night, and it was still pretty chilly, so I huddled up in a nearby blanket. *Mother has really flipped this time,* I thought. My mom has a lot of pizzazz, and she has always been the most ambitious go-getter I have ever known. I could see that the children were shivering in the cold bean field, however, and wondered if she hadn't gone a little too far.

Within half an hour Richard plopped a huge bucket full of beans on the kitchen table, and the children came in with chattering teeth. Then my mother stormed in the door and announced, "I asked one of you to turn the water on for me out there, and you just walked off and left me." Silence hung over the children. They couldn't think of a thing to say.

"And I see that no one put the beans in the water either!" Another silence. We all knew that Grandma was angry!

"Who did you tell to put the beans in the water?" I asked to break the awkward silence, thinking I would really hand out a tongue lashing and relieve the tension.

"The daddy!" she said emphatically.

"Oh," I said, smiling out of the corner of my mouth at a chagrined father looking like a naughty little boy caught in the act.

"Why do you want those beans in the water?" I asked, knowing that was not our usual procedure for putting up beans.

"Don't you know? Didn't anyone tell you?" she asked. "It froze last night! If we hadn't got those beans off the vines before the sun hit them, they would certainly have been ruined!" She continued, "Sometimes if you put water on frozen plants before they warm up, they can be saved."

Suddenly I understood her urgency. The lovely crop of beans she had so carefully planted, weeded, and nurtured all summer long, mostly for our benefit, looked as if it would be totally destroyed because of one cruel, early summer frost. Why hadn't I thought of that? Being away from farm life for many years had dimmed my memory of the horror of the early frosts for which her locale was notorious.

"Well, it looks like you've saved this many anyway," I said, trying to think of something encouraging to say.

"Maybe," she ventured, not yet ready to be too optimistic. She was still upset—primarily at the weather, but also at the children.

Before long, things calmed down a bit, and Saren, Shawni, Saydi, Mom, and I settled down to snap beans.

"What children really need to be taught is how to work," Mom said in her most tactful way. Her statement went right to my very soul. "They need to be taught that work needs to be done whether they like it or not." I wondered how much complaining had taken place in the bean patch, as she concluded, "And they need to be taught to follow through to the end and not just leave loose ends hanging!"

My life seemed to flash before my eyes, and I remembered the many times she had tried to instill that in me when I was growing up.

With snapping beans as background music, she proceeded to tell us about the time when her father had told her to drive a buckrake from one field to another, a chore that required passing over a narrow path bordered on one side by a cliff and on the other by a deep ravine. She was about twelve years old at the time.

"If I had measured, I'm sure there wouldn't have been an inch left over on either side," she said. "But I did it without question, though I was scared to death. I knew that if the rake started to fall, the horse and I would go with it," she explained with great expression and drama.

"Why, when my brother and sister and I were six, seven, and eight, we were put in a big box my dad had made for us on the harrow so we wouldn't fall out, and he left us, with our little lunch bags, to harrow the fields for the day. He left us at dawn and picked us up at dusk." The girls' mouths seemed to fall a little wider open at each successive story.

By the time we finished snapping the beans, the children had a new appreciation for their grandmother. Something else very interesting happened too. After the beans, we put up a bushel of pears, and the children worked like little troopers. There was not one complaint! Occasionally we sent them off to play while we got the next project organized. The minute we called them, they were there with willing hands. I could hardly believe what a great day we had and what a sense of satisfaction the children felt when they showed their father the fruit of their labors at the end of the day.

As the day progressed, Mom and I had a chance to talk a lot about the responsibility of work. She pointed out the many advantages of farm living in teaching children to work. Having taught school for forty years, she said that she could usually tell those children who had lived on farms because of how they tackled their schoolwork.

Knowing that my children would probably never have the opportunity for full-time farm experience, I wondered if I would ever be able to teach them responsibility. However, as I thought further about it, I realized that a farm was not an absolute necessity. Some things are easier to teach on a farm, but others are more easily taught elsewhere.

Therefore, in this chapter we will talk about ways and means to teach responsibility for work regardless of circumstances. We hope some of these ideas fit into your family so that you too can nurture happy children who understand and appreciate the value of work. Incidentally, as evidenced by the previous story, we hope it helps us, too!

B. Methods

1. *Whistle while you work.* (To implant the idea that work can be fun, and that the fulfillment that comes from it is always fun.)

Everyone remembers Tom Sawyer, who made the job of whitewashing a fence appear so attractive that other boys paid him to let them do part of it. The interesting thing about that story is that the boys enjoyed it. They didn't just imagine that it was fun—it actually was fun, because of their attitude.

Small children whose parents enjoy work will accept the responsibilities of work naturally, and even with a degree of ease.

Make a conscious effort to reveal to your children the fulfilling side of work. Tell them how good it feels to get a job done. Tell them how glad you are to have the strength or ability to do a certain job. And yes, if you can bring yourself to do it, sing or whistle while you work.

2. *Family job meeting.* (To help children see the scope of work in a household and to feel the honor of sharing in that work.)

Announce at least a week ahead of time that there will be a special family meeting for everyone old enough to read (probably six and up).

At the meeting, begin by telling the children how much you love them and want to make home a warm and wonderful place for them to live and grow. Then show them a list of things that have to be done to keep home a pleasant place. The list should be big and readable. It might look something like this:

Do shopping	Clean house
Prepare meals	Vacuum
Do dishes	Wash windows

Pick up clutter	Wash car
Make beds	Do laundry
Clean bathrooms	Fix broken things
Clean and wax floor	Drive people places
Mow lawn	Feed pets
Shovel snow	Turn off lights
Trim bushes	Empty dishwasher
Water lawn	Set table
Care for garden	Empty garbage and trash

Then, in your own words and on a level your children can understand, convey the following ideas: "These jobs are important because doing them well makes our house a good home. When children are babies, they aren't old enough to help. But as they get bigger, they are smart enough and strong enough to start doing some of these important things. Which things do you think you are big enough to do?"

Aim your discussion at connecting certain children with certain jobs. Put names by the jobs. There will be four keys to your success:

(a) *Keep it simple.* It is usually better if each child has one or two basic daily jobs and one or two basic weekly jobs. He won't do them if he can't remember them.

(b) Be sure each child knows exactly *how* to do his job. Do it *with* him several times. Show him the finer points. Show him how to take pride in doing it right. He won't do it if he doesn't think he knows how.

(c) *Follow through.* Be sure each child does his assignments every day and every week. Habits take a month or two to develop, and every time he fails to do a job, the habit-forming process is set back almost to the beginning. He won't do it if he doesn't think you'll follow through.

(d) *Make it visible.* Prepare a chart that shows the child's name and his job, and mark it each time he completes the job. (Colored stars may be the easiest and most effective mark.) He won't do it unless he gets reinforcement for it.

Children younger than six can, of course, have little family jobs of their own, but usually do not understand or relate as well to this kind of a discussion.

3. *Ancestor stories.* (To help children see that their ancestors had to work much harder than most people today, and that working was good, and often fun, for them.)

If you have journals or records of your parents or grandparents, and if you can find or remember incidents in their lives involving work, then you may have a powerful opportunity to pass on to your children not only the theory but also the tradition of work.

Tell the incident to your children in simple language. Be sure they understand exactly whom you are talking about and that they are descendants, and therefore part of, that ancestor.

Follow the story with a discussion of the importance and joy of work. You may want to write down the stories you use so that they can be retold periodically.

4. *Take the day off.* (To show children how fast a household can deteriorate when the work isn't done.)

When you have established a clearly defined pattern of family jobs, try this method to impress children with how important all of the jobs are. Pick a day when the children's "weekly jobs" are usually performed; try to choose a day when most of the family will be home for most of the day. Be prepared for a fairly frazzling experience but one that teaches a memorable lesson.

At dinner the night before, surprise the children by saying, "Let's not do any of our family jobs tomorrow. We're tired; let's just take the day off." You'll get some puzzled looks, and also some delighted looks.

Then play it straight and really do nothing the next day. Don't fix any meals or do any dishes; don't sweep any floors or wash any clothes. Tell the children not to wash their basins or empty the garbage or whatever their regular jobs are. When a child wants food (babies excluded, of course), tell him in a friendly way to get his own, that no one is doing any work today.

By evening you'll have a good deal of distemper, some hungry children, a messy house, and a high level of chaos and confusion.

Gather the family together and ask them if they want to do the same thing the next week. They won't. Then have a discussion about the importance of family jobs. Starting with the parents, have each family member commit to do his daily jobs each day and his weekly jobs each week without fail. Then have everyone pitch in and get things back in order.

5. *Job auction.* (To get children involved with work beyond their regular jobs and to teach them the connections between work and rewards.)

Children should be motivated to do their regular jobs as a part of the family, as their fair share, and to gain natural satisfaction. However, it is also a good idea to teach them that many jobs are worth doing not only because they are important, but also because they pay.

Make a list of the things that need doing that are not regularly assigned jobs, and put a price by each of them (such as wax the downstairs floor, seventy-five cents; clean out workbench drawer, fifty cents; and so forth.) Let the children take turns choosing jobs. If a child doesn't want to participate, don't force him. Help him see the difference between regular jobs, which are his responsibility, and optional jobs, which he can do if he wants to earn money. If your children have gained the responsibility for money, as discussed in the last chapter, you'll find that very few jobs will go unclaimed.

Be sure children are paid quickly after they complete a job, either in cash or by credit entry to their "family bank" account (described in the previous chapter). For some jobs a time limit is helpful; for others it is wise to take more time and do the job with precision and pride, emphasizing the satisfaction of quality rather than speed or quantity.

Small children find it difficult to understand anything except immediate rewards (even a smile of approval is a great reward). As children grow older, however, they begin to understand the principle of long-range rewards as well as immediate ones, such as performing in an orchestra because they practiced hard.

Rewards are not only acceptable in a family working together to improve—they are essential!

6. *Build something together.* (To reinforce the pleasure of work by sharing it and having children see your example.)

The summer I was ten, my father, brother, and I built a log cabin in the mountains. We cut the trees, notched the logs, split the shingles, and bricked the fireplace. My father loved the hard work, and I loved it because he did. I've never forgotten the communication of that summer, both verbal and nonverbal.

Whether it's a cabin or a doghouse or a room in the basement, building together is a constructive and valuable endeavor, one that creates in children an honest desire for the responsibility of work.

7. *Have a garden with assigned crops.* (To teach children the law of the harvest, which should be at the heart of their understanding of the responsibility of work.)

As mentioned earlier, my mother could tell which of her schoolchildren had come from farms because of their greater sense of responsibility. A farm environment not only demands a great deal of hard work, it also teaches the invaluable law of the harvest—that one reaps only what he sows. A farm or garden may not be the only way to teach this lesson, but it is probably the most direct and effective way to teach it.

If it is possible, arrange to have a garden. Give each child a plot. Decide together which child will raise which vegetable. It is simpler and often more effective when each child has only one crop.

Tell the children you will help them, and answer their questions when they ask, but help them understand that they are responsible for their own gardens. Then stick with it. Remind them once in a while when watering or weeding is needed, but don't push them. Let the law of the harvest work.

When they do harvest, help them see that they could have had more if they'd worked harder, and less if they had not worked as hard.

8. *The money game.* (To help children understand how cooperation in doing household work can make everyone's job easier.)

Place two chairs at opposite ends of a room. Get a rope long enough to tie around the waists of two family members. You will also need some money—paper or coins, the amount is up to you.

Have two family members stand back to back between the two chairs with one end of the rope tied around each person's waist. Make sure the rope is not long enough that they can walk away from each other and reach both chairs.

Tell them that whoever can get the money on the chair that he is facing—within ten seconds—can keep the money. Then say "go." Start timing. After ten seconds say "stop."

One of two things will happen. Either they will pull against each other trying to get their own money, or they will run first to one chair and then to the other, getting all of the money. If they have pulled against each other, they may have gotten only the money from one chair, or possibly no money at all. Those that have cooperated and have gone first to one chair and then to the other will probably have gotten all of the money in less time.

Have a discussion about cooperating within your family to achieve common goals and how this works to benefit all family members. Give another chance to those teams who did not cooperate the first time. Everyone will then leave the game with money and will have this positive feedback: *If I cooperate I will be rewarded.* (Mention that the reward will not always be a material one.)

C. Family Focal Point: The Pegboard

As in so many families, our efforts to teach our children responsibility for work were mixed successes. Sometimes they seemed to work brilliantly; other times they seemed to be total failures.

We did at one point, however, chance upon a practice that has eliminated this erratic pattern and replaced it with fairly consistent efforts by all of the children to do their parts. We think it has also helped them to feel the joy as well as the responsibility of work.

We had been using a system where the child got a star on the "chore chart" each time he did his job. When he got twenty stars, he was given a reward. What we began to notice was that the reward wasn't really necessary. The *stars* were what the children wanted. They wanted the satisfaction of putting a bright star on the chart by their name. The star symbolized accomplishment, fulfillment, the completion of a task.

That started us thinking. If it was the act of putting on that star that motivated them, how could we expand that motivation by offering them something like a star, only bigger and better? What we came up with was a pegboard. It consists of a two-by-four board (about fourteen inches in length) for each child. Each board has four half-inch holes in it, and four big, blocky wooden pegs are attached to the board with string. Each child's two-by-four has his name carved on it and is attached to the others with dowels. The boards look something like this:

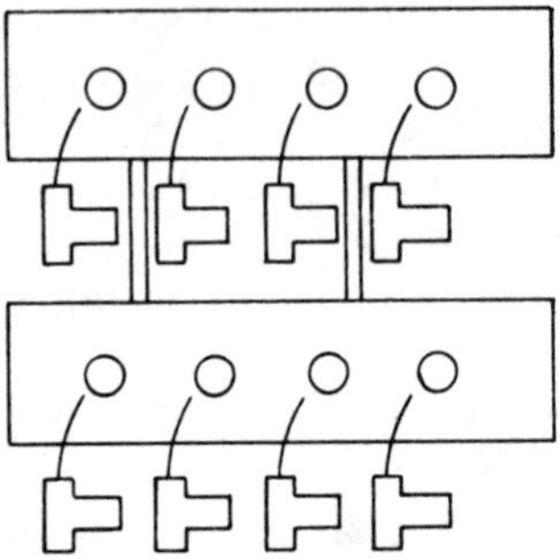

Each peg represents one responsibility that the children have each day and can be pushed into its hole only when that responsibility is fulfilled. In our case the first peg is the "morning peg" and can go in when the child has made his bed, brushed his teeth, and gotten ready for school. The second peg is the "practice peg"; it can go in when the child has done his one hour (half an hour for smaller ones) of music practice for the day. The third peg is the "job peg"; it goes in when the child's daily job is done. The last peg is the "evening peg"; it can go in when the child has put his things away, has laid his clothes out for the next school day, and is ready for bed.

All the jobs can be done before dinner, so it is standard procedure that all pegs must be in place before a child eats (the evening peg is from the evening before).

The interesting thing is that the chief motivation for getting the pegs in is not the threat of having no dinner; it is the satisfaction of the pegs themselves and what they represent. They are big and blocky, and they fit snugly into their holes. It's fun to put them in and fun to look at them after they are in. The children receive praise each evening when they put the last ones in, and they feel good about having taken care of their responsibilities that day.

As an alternative to the wooden pegboard, you might consider a "tag board."

Cover a twelve-by-twenty-four-inch board with colorful but plain contact paper. With stickers put the name of each of your children on the board. Then evenly space cup hooks (about 2½ inches apart) and screw them into the board.

On the front of the tags write what each one represents. On the back of the tag put a sticker of a smiling face or an animal or whatever. As you begin each day, put on the metal-rimmed tags with the "responsibilities" facing out. As each one is completed, the tag is turned over by the child.

Whether you use pegs, stars, or something similar, this visual family focal point can go a long way toward promoting consistency in your children's acceptance of the responsibility for work.

Linda says this:

As parents in a modern society, we often don't realize the benefits of work for our children. We think we are doing them a big favor by doing things for them. We consider them either too young for the responsibility or too old to be bothered with little jobs.

I was making my three-year-old's bed one day, and thinking that she should be making it. Recalling the struggle I had experienced in urging her to make her own bed, I finally decided that it just wasn't worth it to try again. I would make the bed myself. I decided that she was too little and would "grow into it."

I realized later that that decision was probably wrong. Children at ages three and four have a real need to feel responsible. They thrive on responsibility and feel great satisfaction in the doing if they are properly taught how. Too often we tell children to do things we have done many times, and when they don't do them, we fail to realize that it may be because they don't know how.

I recall a conversation with a friend whom I considered to be one of the most responsible people I had ever met. When I asked him about his youth as an only child, he told me that he could not remember being told to do something without help from his mother to accomplish it. It was never, "Go make your bed." It was always, "Let's go make your bed." He learned responsibility as his mother taught him how to do things.

I had only three children at that time, but even then I thought, *That's fine for an only child, but what about mothers who have troops of children?* Making a bed with each child each day didn't seem any more feasible than having a platoon sergeant help each soldier make his bed each day.

As we had more children, however, I realized that it is not only possible but absolutely crucial to help little children learn *how*. It is possible to take time after the older children are off to school to give pointers on things like making beds or cleaning rooms. It helps to remember that we have to accept pretty lumpy beds even at that. I've learned to *ask* my two-year-old if his bed is made before I pass judgment.

The next step is to encourage children to do regularly on their own initiative what they know how to do. After trying many things that didn't work, we decided to have them set their own goals about making their beds, cleaning their rooms, and brushing their teeth. I remember when our four-year-old decided that his goal would be to make his bed every day for a week. Four days out of seven I went into his room in the morning to find, to my amazement, that his bed was already made. On the other three days just a few words to remind him brought immediate results. When I think of all the struggles we have had with children through the years, I am amazed that it took me so long to figure out how to get results: first, teach them *how*; then, let *them* set the goal.

The same principles apply with slightly older children. Since I try to teach several of ours a music lesson each day before school, one of our dilemmas was how to get breakfast prepared at the same time. The only two children not involved in music lessons at the time were the six- and seven-year-olds. One Saturday I spent a couple of hours teaching them how to prepare various breakfast foods. Since then, we've never eaten better. They prepare breakfast every morning. They are much more creative than I am. Their creations are usually very good, and though we all crunch down on an eggshell occasionally, everybody's happy. There's almost nothing those children would rather do than create breakfast!

As children grow older, we assume that they have so many outside responsibilities (homework, ballet lessons, piano practice, Boy Scouts and Girl Scouts, and so forth) that they can't handle any home responsibilities. Often our natural inclination is to think, "I'll do the cooking, dishes, cleaning, and straighten their rooms for them, and leave them to the important things." In the long run, this is the wrong course.

Children should understand that Mother also has many responsibilities. They should know that she too has things that *she* likes to do to improve herself. When there is routine work to be done, everyone should share the responsibility.

It's extremely important for the father to be a part of this understanding and to "rally others to the cause." If he leads the children by willingly and cheerfully helping with dishes and other household chores, then the children will offer far less resistance themselves.

Section 1 Summary Story

Dan and Corry Thompson had read the first section of this book and were trying diligently to implement it with their four children. They had developed a set of family laws and were using the trigger word of "please" to remind children of their responsibility for obedience. They had made a "Gunny Bag" to motivate little children to put their toys away and had adopted a practice of putting out-of-order clothes on the children's beds so that they had to be put away. They had a pegboard to teach children responsibility for their family jobs and daily performance.

They were implementing the methods, and these were working reasonably well, but something still seemed wrong. One evening, as Dan returned from work, he heard Corry directing the children to get their pegs in and clean the things off their beds. It suddenly occurred to him what was wrong with their system. He and Corry were always taking the initiative. The children were following the program when they were *told* to, but they weren't taking the initiative. He and Corry discussed it later that evening and realized that responsibility *is* initiative—that as long as *they* were taking the initiative, *they* still had the responsibility. They hadn't yet given the responsibility for things, for obedience, or for work to their children.

Over the next few weeks they developed a simple system that reversed the initiative and literally gave the responsibility to the children. This is what they did:

1. They got a large, painted wooden box with a lid and a big combination lock. They labeled the box "The Thompsonville Family Bank" and put a slot in the lid.
2. They told the children that they could have ten points for each of their four pegs that they put in the pegboard each day and an additional ten points for being on time and participating in the dinner discussion each evening.
3. The children could fill out a slip each night totaling their

points for the day, get it initialed by mom or dad, and put it in the slot.

4. If laws had been broken or a child had not obeyed during the day, or if his things were out of order, the parent would take off points before initialing the slip.

5. At the end of the week, on Saturday, payday would come. There would be a possibility of 250 points. All points over 200 would be doubled and the children would be paid two cents for every point.

It was completely the responsibility of each child to get his pegs in and to get his slip initialed and into the bank each day. If he failed to do so, nothing was said—he just missed his chance for that day's points.

The system incorporated all three kinds of responsibility taught in the first section of this book and gave the initiative for all three to the children. You might want to try some individually tailored adaptations.

SECTION 2

RESPONSIBILITY TO SOCIETY

Children can learn to recognize man's interdependence and the resulting need to respect each other's rights. Morality thus assumes a logical, practical dimension.

The purpose of this section is to help children feel responsible to society for their actions, their talents, and their attitudes.

The proper combination of love and fear is the key to teaching children responsibility. When love and the positive form of fear are combined, they produce respect, and respect yields responsibility. Children will become truly responsible to parents only when they both love and fear them—fear their disapproval because *they love them, and fear the consequences that consistent parents will provide for irresponsibility. Children will become responsible to themselves only as they both love and fear themselves—fear their power to hurt others and fear missing their opportunities and potential.*

Likewise, children become responsible to society as they learn, on the one hand, to love their fellowmen, and, on the other hand, to fear the penalties of broken societal laws and the damage they could do if they failed to manage their actions, talents, and attitudes.

Responsibility for Actions 4

In the final analysis, the great need in the world is not for more genius, or even for more skill. It is for people willing to accept responsibility for what they do.

A. Definition and Illustration

"Ahhh!" you may say. "Now we're getting down to it—it's my children's *actions* that I want them to be responsible for."

As parents, we usually think in the context of making our children responsible to *us* for their actions, and, to a degree, this is as it should be. Over the long term, however, the real key is to help them see (and to help ourselves see) that it is really society they are responsible to.

Helping them to see that, to feel that, and to respect the rights of others enough to want to be responsible for all that they do is the objective of the ideas discussed in this chapter.

Jason was seven. Just over the six-foot fence in his backyard was a parking lot of an apartment complex. Someone in that parking lot had tossed a paper bag of empty beer bottles over the fence, and Jason found them. For several reasons, not all of which he understood, he took the bottles and tossed them, one by one, back over the fence. Since he couldn't see through the fence, he couldn't see them land. But he could hear the crash, and the whole thing was kind of fun.

That evening a man from the apartment complex rang the doorbell, and Jason, who was downstairs, overheard the man telling his father about a punctured tire. Jason went quietly into his room, put on his pajamas, got in bed, and pretended to be asleep.

His parents, after reassuring the neighbor that they would pay for the tire if it turned out to be their son's doing, sat down to decide how to handle the incident. They realized that they had three challenges: (1) to help Jason tell the truth about the matter (they knew him well enough to be pretty sure what the truth was); (2) to help him feel sorry for what he'd done; and (3) to help him feel enough responsibility for his actions that he wouldn't do something similarly irresponsible in the future. As they thought about it, they realized that it was fortunate that the whole thing had come to their attention after Jason was in bed, when they had time to think it through, rather than while he was still up. Otherwise they might have confronted him without much thought as to how to make it a learning experience.

When Jason came to breakfast the next morning, Dad said, "Son, I noticed a sack of beer bottles. Whoever tossed them into our yard shouldn't have done it, should he."

Jason looked up with a little hope in his eyes and said, "No."

Dad said, "You probably felt like tossing them back over and didn't really stop to think that they might hurt anyone or break something." Jason looked down, but said nothing. "Did you throw them over, son?"

There was a pause, then a quiet, "Yes."

"We're proud of you for telling the truth, son. A man's car ran over one of those bottles and got a flat tire. We're lucky none of the bottles broke a windshield. But we do need to figure out what to do about the flat tire." Dad's arm was around Jason's shoulders now. "Do you feel that you understand what an apology is?"

"Sort of."

"What is it, Son?"

"It's when you're sorry."

"That's part of it. Do you feel sorry about throwing those bottles and puncturing the tire?"

"Yes."

"Well, I'll tell you something, Jason. Apologizing is a magic kind of thing. When someone breaks a law or does something wrong, he has to have a punishment unless he apologizes and tries to make things right again. If someone is truly sorry, and does all he can to correct his mistake and to try not to do it again, he can sometimes be forgiven without being punished. Would you like to try this?"

"Yes."

To cut a long story short, Jason cleaned up the rest of the glass. He saved money from odd jobs to pay for the tire. He asked for and received forgiveness from the car's owner. He promised both his parents and the car owner that he would never throw anything over the fence again.

The process made a far stronger impression on Jason than a punishment would have. He gained the satisfaction of putting things right and the realization that putting things back together is usually much harder than breaking them.

The result was an increase in maturity and in Jason's sense of responsibility for his actions.

Every child has some bad habits and mannerisms that we parents dislike intensely. Interestingly, children usually don't like these any better than we do. If you ask a child what his biggest behavior problem is, he will usually come up with the same conclusion you have.

One of our children thrives on being obedient, following the rules, and carrying out her responsibilities. Her problem is that she seems to lie in wait for the brother or sister who doesn't measure up. Two or three times a day she puts on a scowl and complains bitterly, incessantly, and loudly.

Another child cannot accept constructive criticism in any form. If she suspects that we think she has done something wrong, she sulks and stomps off to cry (especially when she really has done something wrong and she knows it).

Several things can be done about these kinds of behavior problems: (1) Ignore them and hope they go away. (2) Accept the fact that your child is just "that way" and that you'll have to grin and bear it. (3) Become angry with the child. (4) Communicate your concerns and sit down together to work out a way for the child to change his actions and for parents to change their responses. Of course, the fourth solution is essential, yet many of us use the others instead.

We must first identify the problem and then work out a solution that child and parent can work on together. Once children are taught basic principles, they should then be taught that the responsibility for their actions is truly theirs, not ours. We are simply there to help.

Our challenge is to teach children how to cope with actions that are a problem, how to control their anger, and how to handle success and failure. Once they have these tools, we must let them take the responsibility for solutions to problems regarding their actions. Our tendency is to demand our own solutions arbitrarily and without consultation. When children decide what they themselves want their actions to be, the result is miraculous.

B. Methods

1. *Laws.* (To help children realize that keeping laws can make us happy.) The "family laws" discussed in the obedience

chapter are a good starting point in helping children to feel responsible for their actions. Take your family laws chart and place it next to a list you have made of some laws of society. Assemble the children and conduct this kind of a discussion:

"What do we call *these* laws?" (Family laws.)

"Where did we get them?" (We made them.)

"Why did we make them?" (Because our family will be happier if we keep those laws.)

"Now, whose laws are *these?*" (Our world's.)

"Why do we have these laws?" (To help us live together with other people and be happy.)

"If everyone in the world could take or do anything they wanted, even if it hurt someone else, would we be happy?" (No.)

Go through the list of society's laws together and talk about how keeping each one brings happiness, and how breaking each one brings unhappiness.

2. *Positive reinforcement.* (To strengthen children's tendencies toward honesty and appropriate actions through the sheer weight of the attention and positive recognition it brings them.)

While it may be too general to call a technique, reinforcement is the most powerful means that parents have to develop children's feelings of responsibility. Praise every incident of honesty, of politeness, of sharing, of good decision making. Make the praise direct and clear. Look the child in the eyes and tell him how proud you are of that action. Then take the compliment beyond that one incident by telling him that he is *that kind of person.* ("You are an honest boy." "You remember to say thank you so much better than you did last year." And so forth.)

If there is one simple and profoundly important truth about children, it is that they live up to their reputations. They will do what they think is actually expected of them. If you can control what *they* think *you* think of them, you can control their actions.

3. *Four-facet review.* (To pinpoint in advance the kinds of behavior problems a child is likely to be most susceptible to.)

As part of the "four-facet review" (discussed in more detail in chapter 5), take time to discuss the behavioral problems of each child. This is a good way to begin the review. Then, as you review the physical, mental, emotional, and social progress of each child, you may well discover some of the reasons or sources of the behavior problems.

The beauty of this approach is the fact that recognizing a behavior problem, defining it, and finding its source go a long way toward solving it.

4. *The consequence game.* (To help children realize that doing what is right is best in the long run.)

Prepare in advance some simple three-by-five-inch index cards with certain dilemmas on one side and the long-term consequences of the choices on the other side. For example, here is a typical dilemma:

> Card 1 (front)
>
> Don't tell your mother that you ate the cookies. She blames your little sister, and you get away with the lie.

Have the child who is "it" pick one option card or the other. When the cards are turned over, they reveal the long-term consequences of each decision.

> Card 1 (back)
>
> No one trusts you because you tell lies.

Other examples of cards follow. You will want to come up with some of your own that fit the actual concerns and potential behavior problems of your own children.

Discuss with your children how the short-term consequences of the wrong choice usually seem pretty good, but that the long-term consequences usually catch up with you.

5. *Two kinds of mistakes.* (To help slightly older children feel responsible not only for *not* doing wrong things, but for *doing* more right things.)

Card 1 (front)

Look across the aisle to Susan's desk and copy her test answers. You get an A on the test.

Card 1 (back)

You will never learn much in school. You will always do badly on tests where you can't cheat. You will get caught sometimes, and people will know that you cheat. Your only friends are other people who cheat.

Card 2 (front)

Don't cheat; just do your own best on the test. Prepare better next time. You get a D on the test, so your parents are mad at you.

Card 2 (back)

You will study harder and do better on the next test. People will trust you, and you will like yourself.

Card 1 (front)

Lie in bed a little longer. It's cold and you're tired. Mom thinks you're sick and lets you stay home from school.

Card 1 (back)

You have a lazy day where you don't learn much of anything. You feel like a lazy person who never gets much done.

Card 2 (front)

Get right up and get your school things together. You do your household jobs and get right off to school on time.

Card 2 (back)

Your actions make for a happy, alert day where you learn a lot and feel good.

Card 1 (front)

Ignore the old lady who needs the snow shoveled. Go skiing instead.

Card 1 (back)

You become a selfish person who always thinks of himself and never of others. The only friends you have are the ones who want something from you.

Card 2 (front)

Go and shovel her sidewalks. You miss a great ski trip.

Card 2 (back)

You learn the joy of service. You serve others and find that others serve you and love you.

Card 1 (front)

Try the cigarette Bobby has. The other kids pat you on the back and think you're neat.

Card 1 (back)

No one really respects you because you're afraid to stand up for what you believe.

Card 2 (front)

Tell Bobby you would never smoke a cigarette and don't think that he should either. The other kids call you a chicken and tell you to "get lost."

Card 2 (back)

Kids start to look up to you. Some of *them* decide not to smoke anymore because they want to follow your example.

Tell, in your own words, the following story:

Bill had the worst day of his life. He was called to the principal's office twice in one day.

The first time was in the morning. Tommy had brought a pair of pliers to school, and he and Bill took the bolts out of the teeter-totter at recess just before two little girls sat on it. The teeter-totter came apart, and the girls skinned their knees. The principal gave them a lecture they would never forget. He said, "Bill, there are certain things you must *not* do!"

Then that afternoon, Bill was called in again. This time it was because he hadn't done his math homework all week. The principal said, "Bill, there are certain things you *must* do!"

Have a discussion with the children about the two kinds of mistakes—one is "doing wrong things," the other is "not doing right things." Give them several examples of bad actions or mistakes, and see if they can determine which category each one fits into. You might use the "wrong choice" cards from the consequence game (method 4 in this chapter).

6. *Erasing the black marks.* (To simplify the concept of apologizing and to show how it applies to the two kinds of mistakes.)

On a sheet of lined paper, write two or three randomly chosen names. (Be sure they are not the names of children whom your children know.) Then, using the "wrong choice" cards from the consequence game, connect a mistake with one of the names on your sheet of paper (for example, Julie looked on someone else's paper and cheated on a test). With a soft pencil, make a black mark by Julie's name. Then say:

"Julie made a mistake. Which kind of mistake was it—doing something wrong, or not doing something right? When we make mistakes, it's as though we have a black mark. If we want to get rid of those marks, we must apologize and try to make things right. How could Julie apologize for cheating?" (She can tell her teacher what she did and that she doesn't deserve the A. She can say she is sorry and promise never to do it again.) "If she did all that, her black mark would be erased."

Erase Julie's black mark and repeat the process with one of the other names and one of the other "wrong choice" cards. Each time be sure the children understand that apologizing is difficult and often embarrassing, but that one feels much better afterward. Be sure each discussion of "what would she have to do to make things right" includes apologizing, making restitution, and promising not to do it again.

7. *Teaching with consistency.* Once again, the secret to success in teaching our children to act in a certain way or to change their actions is our own consistency.

A simple illustration comes to mind. One of the most impressive traits about British children is their consistent habit of saying "please" and "thank you." During the three years our family spent in England, I seldom heard a child ask for or receive anything without a "please" or "thank you." When there was a rare miss, the parent always delivered a gentle reminder. Courtesy is a national tradition.

Sentences begin with "please": "Please may I have more milk?" Likewise, a thank-you is given after each small service. A little friend never left our door after an afternoon at play without saying, "Thank you for having me."

In contrast, we recently took nineteen American children, ranging in age from one to ten, in our van to a pumpkin patch to pick their own Halloween pumpkins. The trip took half an hour each way.

The children had a wonderful time, but by the time we returned with nineteen kids and nineteen pumpkins, we were all happy to scramble out! The trip had taken considerable time that we could have used to do other things. The baby was screaming, hungry, and miserable all the way home, and the gas tank was seriously depleted. But not one child thought to say thank you.

Unknowingly and unwittingly, we Americans teach our children to be what the British would consider rude and selfish. Most of us would like our children to be polite, but perhaps we do not desire it enough to pay the price of consistency.

Children do exactly what is expected of them. We have had young women from England living with us for short periods of time on a couple of occasions. By the time they left to return home, our children were markedly more polite. However, as the reminders stopped, so did the children's habit of speaking more politely.

The lesson is a simple one—but by no means easy. Children's actions are changed only by regular reminders, consistent praise, and positive reinforcement.

C. Family Focal Points: "Bathroom Chats," Laws and Apologizing, Code Words

Several years ago, while Richard was a graduate student and our oldest daughter was just beginning to talk, he wanted to begin having regular, private talks with her. Since our small student apartment had only one private room in it, these little meetings took on the title "bathroom chats." They have since become traditional (now occurring elsewhere, but still called "bathroom chats" by the older children). One purpose of the chat is to talk about each child's talents and reinforce his individuality (see chapter 5). As chapter 9 will discuss, it also creates a setting in which the child may talk about monthly and weekly goals. The third purpose of these private chats applies to this chapter.

What we do is to ask each child six or older what he thinks is the main thing he needs to improve in. Amazingly, children usually know, and if the atmosphere of trust is right, they will bring up the very thing you want them to. A child will say, "I need to be more careful to always tell the truth," or, "I need to stop fighting with Saydi." How quickly he comes to his main problem depends partly on how well you have made him aware of it. But once he (through whatever hints and prods you need to give) identifies a problem, it becomes his goal to change it, with your help, rather than vice versa. The weekly (some say monthly is more realistic), repetitive nature of the individual chats allows follow-through and allows you to help your child see that it *is* possible to change and improve. We often put a "code letter" on the back of the child's hand to help him remember the problem he is trying to correct. Also, because there is only *one* problem as opposed to all the good things we have discussed, the child feels self-esteem and doesn't lose confidence because of the single problem.

To get the problems even more "out on the table," we sometimes devote a family meeting to letting each child tell the family what he has decided he needs to work hardest on. Other family members then encourage him, praise him for having the courage to say it, and promise to help.

Of course, the family laws are the heart of responsibility for actions. Family laws, properly used and enforced, can be a prototype or training ground for children's abilities to keep society's laws.

Often, all that children need is a quick and subtle reminder of the need to pay more attention to the correctness of their actions. We have developed some simple codes that we use as reminders in our family. They are particularly useful when we are in someone else's home, or when others are in our home and a direct reminder might embarrass our children. When we want to remind them that their behavior is wrong in some way, we give them a "thumbs up" hand sign. When we want them to look around and see what needs doing, we give them the "OK" sign where thumb touches the index finger. This is an "eye" sign, which means, "Look around and see what needs to be done here." We also have some verbal codes, such as, "Did you remember to send that letter?" This means, "There is someone here that you don't know, and you should get acquainted." When we get a child's attention and clear our throat, we mean "Remember your manners." Each family could develop its own signs and codes; children often respond better to subtle reminders than to major, overt corrections.

If some of the teaching methods in this chapter help your children to feel a sense of responsibility to others for their actions, and to learn how to "erase" their mistakes by apologizing and making restitution, your family will then be in a position where some form of regular behavior review, coupled with some code words and an ongoing growth process, will build genuine responsibility for actions into your children.

5 Responsibility for Talents and Gifts

The best things in life are free, simply because they are the potentials with which we were born.

A. Definition and Illustration

Gifts!

The word conjures images of packages tied with ribbons on birthdays or other special occasions. But how much more the word can mean—the gifts of talents and potential.

The best things in life are free, simply because they are the gifts of life itself. The earth, the sky, our bodies, the plants that grow, our abilities and talents—these are just the start of an endless list of gifts.

Mark was nine. For nearly six years his parents had been aware that he had exceptional conceptual and artistic gifts. When he was three, he could draw shapes and make numbers and letters with surprising accuracy. By the time he started school, he was drawing animals and trees that looked like the product of a child at least five years older. His parents arranged private art lessons for him that year. All went well, and the praise and recognition that Mark's drawing brought him kept him motivated and happy.

Then a year later, a couple of things happened. First, Little-League soccer and baseball started. Then two or three of Mark's peers decided that drawing and art were for girls and sissies, and they voiced this opinion in many not-very-nice ways to Mark. The situation claimed everybody's attention one day when Mark came home from school and announced to his mother, first, that he was no longer an artist—he was a ball-player, and second, that he didn't intend to draw anything again as long as he lived.

Meanwhile, as Mark's story was unfolding, another story was taking place. Mark's little brother Tommy, two years younger, had been living in Mark's shadow. While everyone had been exclaiming over Mark's obvious and visible talent, everyone was wondering just where Tommy's talent was. It was easier to see where Tommy's talents *weren't.* He certainly couldn't draw. He showed no particular musical or athletic aptitude, and his life had consisted mostly of looking for (and having others look for) some gift or ability to parallel Mark's. It hadn't been found. Tommy was basically an average child who spent most of his spare time playing with the little girl and boy next door.

Mark's sudden announcement eventually became a blessing in disguise. It caused his parents, Bill and Marge Caine, to focus on the whole question of talents or the lack of them in both boys. After a long discussion, Bill summarized the problem to his wife. "Marge, it's simple—we have one untalented boy and one talented one who doesn't like his talent. We might be doing something right, but I'd hate to have to try and name it."

But the situation and the discussion represented a turning point. Both Bill and Marge began to think more directly about their responsibility to help their children discover what their positive attributes were, both the obvious and the nonobvious ones, and to help them gain a sense of their responsibility and opportunity to develop them.

In this frame of mind, they began to see Tommy in a new light. They recognized that he had several gifts that had not been apparent to them before. Among them was a rather remarkable ability to teach and influence small children. Tommy's "play" with the two children next door consisted mostly of teaching them games and telling them stories. He had a beautiful and compassionate way with little children. They also noticed that Tommy had an exceptional ability to persevere. He could work at something much longer than Mark. He followed through. He didn't feel right until a thing was done. For a child, he was unusually dependable. He wasn't brilliant or quick at learning, but his attention span was long. He made up for his lack of quickness with his tenacity. It was through talking together about Tommy that his parents began to notice these qualities.

As they recognized them, they found themselves being more complimentary toward Tommy, praising him more, pointing out to him how good he was at certain things. Tommy flourished under the praise, and Mark started looking for ways to win back his old monopoly on his parents' compliments. He even started drawing again. The parents responded by redoubling the praise of Mark's talent. They took him to museums. They checked out library books about great artists. They found material on people who were both artists and athletes. They made a conscious effort not only to praise Mark's art, but also to praise art itself.

While living in Washington, D.C., we were invited to attend a concert given by the Yamaha School of Music at the Kennedy Center. Because we encountered difficulties in finding a baby-sitter, we came within a hair's breadth of not going, but we will be forever grateful that we did.

Two nine-year-olds, two eleven-year-olds, one fourteen-year-old, and one fifteen-year-old were to perform their own compositions. "How good can this be?" we wondered as we reflected on the skill level of our own nine-year-old.

As the children were introduced, they looked just like any other children. The nine-year-old girls were dressed in lovely pastel dresses and lacy white anklets and Mary Jane shoes.

As the first nine-year-old took her seat at the piano, she carefully placed her hands in her lap and then held them above the keys, poised to begin. We were still not prepared for what we were to hear. After the first minute our mouths dropped open. Her own original composition seemed just short of miraculous. We couldn't believe that what we were hearing was not an adult virtuoso.

It went from miraculous to even better as the second nine-year-old took her place at a huge synthesizer similar to an organ, with several keyboards and a hundred or so stops and foot pedals. By intermission, when each child had performed an astounding original composition, we were heartsick that our children and parents and everyone else we knew were not there to see and hear it.

After the intermission, three of the youngsters again performed original pieces, but this time with the Washington National Symphony under Rostropovitch, the great maestro and cellist. Again we could hardly believe what we were hearing.

Then, as though that were not enough, all the children were seated at the front of the stage for the last section. Volunteers from the audience were then asked to play a two-measure theme on the piano. The children were to use those eight or ten notes as the basis of a three- to four-minute spontaneous composition, using proper chord structure, rhythm, and harmony. Volunteers did come forward and did play short, eight-note melodies previously unheard by the children. Each child, in turn, took the theme and turned it into a beautiful four- or five-minute rendition.

To ice the cake, before the last theme was presented, the request from the moderator was that the composition be a duet! The two nine-year-olds quickly volunteered, one on the piano, the other on the synthesizer, and their performance brought those in the audience to their feet shouting "Bravo! Bravo!"

Every person in that concert hall went home with a new appreciation of children and their talents. We went home more convinced than ever of the responsibility each person has to develop the gifts he is given.

Those children were obviously prodigies, yet we wished we could have studied their backgrounds. They must have come from families who were keenly aware of their children's gifts and had searched for the best way to develop them. Because the children evidenced such serenity and enthusiasm, I'm sure the children felt that they had a special gift at a very early age, and they were determined to do something about it!

Though we realized that not many children are as gifted, we certainly left that auditorium understanding that our children's potential was much greater than we had given them credit for. We recommitted ourselves that night to look harder for the real talents of our children and to help them develop their own appreciation for those gifts along with a deeper feeling of responsibility for their development.

B. Methods

1. *Four-facet review.* (To help parents recognize children's gifts and become aware enough of them to help their development.)

Do what Mr. and Mrs. Caine did: set aside some time to think together about each child. Talk about his physical, mental, emotional, and social capacities. Prompt each other's thinking. Ask each other what you have noticed about each of the facets of each child. Take notes. Analyze.

Here's a promise: you'll *discover* things about your children—their character, their talents, their potential—in this kind of a one-on-one brainstorming discussion that neither of you has ever thought of before.

Here's another promise: you'll enjoy it! And you will think of specific things to do that will be important in the development of your children's gifts. Do it at least once a month.

2. *A simple nature walk.* (To help small children appreciate the works of nature and begin to feel responsible for taking care of them.)

Few things are as exhilarating as taking a walk in the outdoors with a child. The early spring or late autumn may be the best time, but any season is wonderful. He will show you more than you show him. If he doesn't point, follow his eyes.

Help him appreciate what he sees. Reinforce his natural capacity for noticing things and his sensitivity to beauty. Pick up litter as you go. Talk about how important it is to care for the earth, and how good it makes us feel to see our world clean and beautiful.

3. *Records.* (To help children appreciate their bodies and see how use of them can improve how well they work.)

Set up a series of four or five physical events, such as a fifty-yard dash, a standing broad jump, or a tennis-ball throw. Time or measure each child's performance in each event and record it in a family scrapbook or a bulletin board chart; explain that you'll do it again in a couple of weeks. Show the children how they can practice to improve their records. Be sure you emphasize that they are practicing to improve their own best, that they are competing only against themselves. Offer prizes to anyone who breaks his own record at the next "meet." Discuss how our bodies grow healthier as they are exercised and as muscles grow stronger.

4. *Loans.* (To help children understand the idea of having something being loaned to them, with the promise that if they take care of it, they may later have it for their own.)

Think of something that your child wants and that you have been planning to get him. Whatever it is, loan it to him rather than giving it. Say, "Johnny, this tennis racket is mine. I bought it with my money, and it belongs to me. I think you should have one, but I want to be sure you can take care of a tennis racket. I'm going to let you use this racket and take care of it for me. It will be just as though it's yours except that I'll take it back if you don't take care of it. You should always keep it in its place, always put the cover on it when you're not using it, and spray the strings each week so they won't get dry and break. If you take really good care of it, I will give it to you."

Then follow up. Remind him often. You want to give the racket to him, so be sure he succeeds. After a couple of weeks, praise him extensively and give him the racket.

As you are giving it to him, explain that this is exactly the way that the world works. The beautiful earth and our talents are here for us to use, but if we don't take good care of them, we may lose them. If we do work hard to care for the earth and to develop our abilities, we will have joy in these things throughout our lives.

5. *Horizon-expanding methods.* (To help children realize that there are a great many interesting aspects to life and that they have the power to explore and to discover their own talents and interests.)

(a) *Interesting things at dinner.* You can instigate a good, around-the-table discussion at dinner time by saying, "Let's all think for a moment about the most interesting thing we saw or heard or had happen to us today. When you've thought of something, put your knife in front of your plate. When everyone has one, we'll go around the table and hear them all."

This can become a fascinating daily tradition. As it unfolds, it will give you opportunities to notice where your children's interests and abilities lie and to encourage their further development.

(b) *New experiences.* In connection with method *a* above, find ways to encourage your children to try new things to see if they are good at them or interested in them. Help them see that trying new experiences is the only way to find out how good we might be at them. Encourage them to volunteer for a service project, to try out for a school play, and so forth.

(c) *Early bedtime and reading.* Children as well as parents usually waste the golden hours between dinner and bedtime. Too much television is watched while too few constructive discussions or experiences or learning-oriented activities occur. One way to improve on this time is a bedtime policy where the children go to bed an hour before the time you think they should be asleep. If you can supply them with library books that will catch their interest and expand their vision, the hour can become a timely, valuable one. The most direct and effective way to do it is simply to set the hour-earlier bedtime and then tell the children that they can choose between going right to sleep and reading for an hour. Even nonreaders will choose to read when given such alternatives. This policy will work only if you are willing to exert the effort to help find genuinely interesting reading material for each child. If you include your children in the library search, you will gain a bonus advantage—additional insight into their likes and dislikes.

C. Family Focal Points: Four-facet Review, Family Tree, Experts Board, Gift Abbreviations, Family Garden

We have found several of the foregoing methods fruitful and fun enough that we carry them on beyond the particular month that we are concentrating on responsibility for gifts. The "early bedtime and reading" policy has become a pleasure for us all, as has the "interesting things at dinner" discussion period.

There are two or three even more basic practices that we would like to suggest to help you instill the responsibility for gifts in your children's minds, procedures you may find you are able to do regularly without any great commitment of time or energy.

Linda and I have a special date once each month, usually to a quiet restaurant that lends itself to thoughtful conversation. There we hold our "four-facet review" (method 1 from this chapter). We always come home with more insight into each child and with more specific ideas about how to help each.

We have a "family tree" on our wall with pictures of the children's grandparents, great-grandparents, and great-great-grandparents. From journals we have extracted short stories about several of them that are both entertaining and illustrative of their personalities and gifts. We have looked for talents in these ancestors that are similar to some of the talents we see in our children. The children, in seeing those connections, are reinforced both in their appreciation of their gifts and in the responsibility for development that is implied.

On the wall of our playroom we also have a "family experts board," divided into thirty or forty small squares, each noting one particular gift of a certain child. For instance, "Saydi—good at singing harmony." "Talmadge—good at doing somersaults." The board is updated as children mature and as new gifts become evident.

A related practice came about one day quite by chance. Six-year-old Josh, who soaks up praise and compliments like a sponge, got so excited as I was telling him what he was good at that he said, "Write those good things down, Dad!"

"Where shall I write them, Josh?"

He looked around, smiled, and said, "On my hand!"

He wanted those good things where he could see them,

where he could be reminded of how good he was. So I did; I wrote on one finger "math," on another "art," on another "fixing things." He didn't want to wash his hand!

The next week he wanted to do it again. We simplified it to a small abbreviation on the tip of each finger. By the following week, all of the children wanted the same thing, and it became a weekly tradition. I now use a pen with ink that washes off easily, and I'm still amazed at how those little visual symbols of individual gifts make children feel happier, more secure, and more inclined to be responsible to use and develop their talents.

One final method—a common and obvious one, but one that is very effective—is a family garden. We let each child be responsible for one separate crop. If they weed and water it, they get results; if they don't weed and water it, they don't reap the reward. The law of the harvest is obvious and graphic to them. We try to apply the lesson to all of life's gifts. If they are cared for, they grow; if not, they don't.

6 Responsibility for a Peaceful Attitude

The greatest challenge of mankind is to create peace within the world. The greatest challenge of an individual is to create peace within himself.

A. Definition and Illustration

Something we greatly admire in Japanese society is its emphasis on harmony. Children are taught that the cardinal offense is the breaking of harmony. Through example and through expectations, parents can bequeath to their children the gift of calmness and a peaceful attitude, and can teach them that they are just as responsible for their emotions as they are for their actions.

James was an hour late getting home from school. He was only six, and his puffy eyes told his mother that there was a rather unpleasant reason for his lateness. They sat down together, and James explained, "I walked home with Tommy because he said it was on my way. But after he went into his house I started walking and couldn't remember where my house was. I started going back to Tommy's but then I couldn't find his house either. All the houses looked the same, so I started to cry. There was no one around to help me. Then I remembered what you told me about being calm. I sat down and just tried to think quietly. After a minute I could think better, and I saw Jensons' house at the end of the road, and I remembered that our road was the next one over."

The responsibility for a peaceful attitude is not only a great parental teaching obligation—it is also a great opportunity to place our children, as they mature, more and more in control of their own emotions and thus more and more out of the realm of our care.

As we attempt to bring this great force into our lives, we find that, in several ways, meeting this responsibility facilitates the meeting and teaching of all the other forms of responsibility. When children have inner peace, they become teachable, calm, and far more responsible, in general, than they are or can be without it.

Many spend large amounts of time and money trying to learn the principle of meditation, of relaxation response. But small children can not only experience calm but come to feel responsible for it, if taught by the simple methods that follow.

B. Methods

1. *Approaches for helping children recognize a peaceful attitude.*

(a) *Feeling something real.* (To help children understand that inside feelings are as real as outside things.)

Gather the children around a popcorn popper; any kind will do, but a hot-air popper works especially well because it is easy to watch.

Make a batch of popcorn. While doing so, stress the senses you are using. Call attention to the sight of the popping corn; the sound of its explosions; the smell; the touch of the rough, warm kernels; and finally, the taste of the kernels, first without salt, then with salt, then with butter.

When all the children have had some popcorn, seat them in a circle in a new location and ask them about each of the senses they experienced. Ask: "What did you see?" "What did you smell? Taste? Touch? Hear?" Explain that these are their senses.

Then tell them that you are going to talk about something we can't taste, touch, smell, see, or hear, but that is just as real as popcorn—our feelings.

(b) *Which would you rather feel?* (To help children want to feel calm and peaceful.)

If you have a puppy or a docile dog, use it for this demonstration. If not, use the softest, warmest stuffed animal you can find.

Blindfold one or more of the children. Have them each feel the puppy or stuffed animal. Talk about how it feels (warm, soft, nice). Then have the children feel an ice cube. Talk about how it feels (cold, hard). Have them feel something rough and unpleasant like sandpaper. Then take the blindfolds off and talk about the differences in how things feel.

Ask the children how they feel when their mother or father gives them a big hug (warm, happy). Tell them that when we are kind to one another or do right things, we have that same kind of feeling—calm, warm, nice. We feel peaceful and happy.

(c) *Three things that rhyme and that help create a peaceful attitude.* (To help children understand the connection between doing right and feeling good.)

Set up a chalkboard or use a large sheet of paper. Give three small sheets of paper to each child. Tell the children that they are going to learn to read three important words, and that the three words all rhyme. Tell them that the amazing thing about the three words is that they each help us to have a peaceful attitude.

On the large paper or chalkboard write, vertically, 1, 2, 3. Next to *1*, write *Aware*. Tell the children what it says, and that to be aware is to pay attention to what you are doing and feeling. If they are upset or frightened or angry at someone, if they can stop and be aware of those feelings, they can calm themselves down. Remind them of how much nicer it is to feel peaceful inside. Have them draw a picture of a child sitting and thinking.

Reinforce the idea that being aware is just *one* way to have a peaceful attitude. Then say, "What else can help us to feel peaceful besides being aware?" By the number *2*, write *Share*. Have the children look at the word and say it for several moments. Explain the word. Have them say *aware* and *share*, and point out that they sound the same, or rhyme.

Do some short role-playing on sharing. For example, have two children who want the same toy yell and fight over it. Then have them start over, but this time they will take turns. When do they feel mad and sad? When do they feel happy and peaceful?

Ask: What made us feel peaceful and happy? (When we shared.)

Tell the children that we now know two sure ways to get a peaceful feeling, and they rhyme. Can you read them? *Aware* and *share*.

Have each child draw a picture of two children sharing. Then say, "There is another sure way to feel peaceful, and it rhymes too." Write *Care* by the number *3* on the paper or board.

Explain that when someone needs help, there are two things we can do: one is to care and help them; the other is to *not* care and not help them.

Make two signs on small pieces of paper. One says *care*, the other says *care* with a line through it to cross it out. Pin the signs on two of the children. Then role-play several simple situations in which a third child pretends to need help (can't take his coat off, lost his nickel, can't put a lid back on something). The child wearing the sign with the word *care* crossed out walks past the one needing help. The one with the care sign stops and helps. Then ask, "Which one made you smile and feel good?" (The "care" one.) What does *care* mean? (To help.) Have the children draw a picture of someone who is caring.

Review again the fact that feelings are real and that peaceful feelings are desirable. Then go back to the list of three words and point at them over and over until the children can read them in unison. Then ask, "How can we get a peaceful feeling?"

Reemphasize that there are three main ways, that they all rhyme, and that they all work: *aware, share, care.*

Hang the sign with the three words on the wall and refer to it often. "Can you remember the words? What happens when we do them?" (We feel peaceful.)

2. *Programming yourself to be calm.* (To help you, as a parent, to radiate the kind of contagious calm that rubs off so effectively onto your children.)

Children are exceptionally accurate mirrors. When we are frustrated or nervous and anxious for any reason, our children will, quite predictably, follow suit and become stubborn, whiny, obstinate, or irritable. It does little good to teach them that they are responsible for how they act unless we set the proper example.

Our common mistakes are: (1) to bring outside frustrations into the home and let them affect our children; and (2) to react thoughtlessly to a child's misbehavior in a way that sets no better example for him than he is setting for us.

Both mistakes can be corrected by programming yourself to be calm and peaceful. The process is simple. Find a particular moment, a certain time each day, when you can decide in advance to react with control and calm to whatever family situations arise. For most parents, the best time is early, before the fast pace of the day takes over. Set aside five minutes alone, perhaps in the bath or shower or just in your room before you emerge to face the day. Let the day's schedule pass through your mind. Think of the little irritations that are likely to arise: the spilled milk, two children demanding attention at the same time, the fighting over a toy—you'll know what they are from experience. Make up your mind to react calmly when they occur. *Decide in advance.* We usually don't decide how we'll react until we are *in* a situation. The key to avoiding a less-than-calm response is to decide how we will react before the situation occurs.

C. Family Focal Points: Morning Quiet Time, Dinner-Hour Calm, Traditions

While there are many appropriate and wonderful ways to help children accept their responsibility for maintaining a peaceful attitude, we focus most of our efforts in three distinct areas: early morning, dinner time, and traditions.

1. *Early morning.* The way in which a day is started often has an influence on the mood and feeling of the entire day. In the Eyre family, we find that if we can begin our days with a calm, quiet, loving feeling, the battle is more than half won. Our older children practice violin and piano before breakfast and school. Our pattern and tradition is that everyone must speak very softly as he gets up and goes about his practicing. When someone speaks loudly or crossly, a finger to the lips is our signal to remember that it is quiet time. When it is time for breakfast, we call the children's attention to the calm feelings that we have felt already that morning and express our hope that they will carry these feelings with them the rest of the day.

2. *Dinner time.* We insist that dinner time also be a time of peace and calm. It is fine for children to be excited about school, or about the ball game that night, or whatever, but they must express this enthusiasm quietly and must talk in turn.

We have a big brass bell that summons the family to dinner. We have tried to arrange the dinner hour so that everyone can be there, and the children know that they must be in their chairs within sixty seconds of the bell's ring. All are asked to think for a moment of the most interesting thing they saw, heard, or had happen to them during the day. (See chapter 5.) The discussion is a peaceful one, and the rule is that anyone who disturbs that mood receives warning and then, on a second violation, has to go to his room until he is ready to behave calmly and peacefully.

3. *Traditions.* We have several traditional weekly activities that we believe help teach this form of responsibility and also make our family stronger.

(a) We have a weekly goal-setting period (see chapter 9)

and talks (see chapter 5). These help the children to be *aware* of their feelings and actions.

(b) We read one or two ancestor stories (see chapter 3).

(c) We decide as a family on one "secret service" that we will perform during the coming week, some act of service or kindness that we can do anonymously.

Each of these practices seems to have a calming, unifying influence on our family. They also offer many opportunities to reinforce with the children how wonderful it is to have calm, good, peaceful feelings.

Section 2 Summary Story

Of all the forms of responsibility in this book, those in this section were most important to Corry and Dan Thompson. They were moral people and felt that if their children were responsible for their actions, their gifts, and their attitudes, their lives would be good as well as happy.

In accordance with the suggestion in the book, they focused on one responsibility per month. During the month they were working on actions, they noticed definite improvement in their children's behavior. The next month they focused on talents and saw clear progress in their children's awareness and appreciation of their individual gifts and uniqueness. The following month the emphasis was on calmness and peace, and again the results were noticeable.

The problem—which became more apparent every month—was that the responsibilities weren't "sticking." No sooner was the focus or emphasis removed from a particular form of responsibility than it began to fade in the children's minds (along with all of its positive effects).

The Thompsonville Family Bank had helped a great deal to give continuity and permanence to the responsibilities of section 1, and Corry and Dan were searching for some equally effective symbol or device to give "staying power" to the responsibilities of section 2.

Because of Dan's hectic work schedule, it was difficult for him to give Corry as much help with the children as he (or she) would have liked. It was difficult, with the exception of weekends, to even predict when he would be at home.

Because the weekend was the one dependable family time,

the Thompsons committed themselves to two objectives to be carried out over each weekend:

1. An individual goal-setting session for the week ahead followed by a talk with Dad in which goals and talents would be discussed.

2. A family discussion (at dinner) of family laws and of important decisions that any family member was facing. This was also an opportunity for everyone to relate any instance during the past week when he had felt particularly calm or peaceful.

They also decided to add two additional features to the Thompsonville Family Bank. One was to get actual checkbooks for the children so they could write out checks (to Mom or Dad) whenever they wanted to withdraw from their account and turn in deposit slips with any extra money they wanted to put in. Second, they decided that the bank would pay an exorbitant rate of interest (40 percent—10 percent each quarter) to give the children a high incentive to save.

These things turned out to be quite easy to do, yet they ensured continuing thought and talk about the responsibility for actions, for gifts, and for a peaceful attitude. The banking additions not only gave the children added responsibility for money, they gave a great *metaphor* for the idea of taking care of talents and environment so they will grow, rather than abusing or neglecting them.

SECTION 3

RESPONSIBILITY TO SELF

A study at a major university attempted to delineate the factors involved in the typical person's ability to translate the acceptance of an idea into the implementation or application of that idea, to motivate us to turn thought into action. The results were as follows:

Step	*Probability of Implementation*
1. Hear an idea that you like	*10%*
2. Consciously decide to adopt the idea	*25%*
3. Decide when you will do it	*40%*
4. Plan how you will do it	*50%*
5. Commit to someone else that you will do it	*65%*
6. Have a specific future appointment with the person you committed to, at which time you will report to him whether you have done it	*95%*

The awakening of the inner motivation and strength of self-discipline is what this section is about.

7 Responsibility for Choices

"If we could only make our children's decisions for them!" we say. But we can't. In the long perspective all we can do—and it is a great deal—is to teach them how to decide for themselves.

A. Definition and Illustration

One of the ironies of life is that the most important and crucial decisions are thrust at us long before we have the wisdom to make them. Before we are a third of the way through life, we usually have to make some of the most far-reaching decisions of our entire lives—marriage, field of study, occupation, location—along with the even more important continuing decisions of values, morality, life-style, and priorities.

By the time children are ten or eleven years old, sometimes even earlier, factors important to these later decisions become evident. Those whom they choose for friends, what they decide to experiment with, which activities they devote interest and time to, whom they look up to and idolize, what they decide about their own status as leader or follower—these and many other choices begin to materialize and to shape the even larger decisions soon to come.

Children who can recognize the connections between what they decide now and what they will *be* later on, who begin to feel responsible for their own choices will greatly increase their chances to make mature and far-sighted decisions that create a foundation for a happy life. Such is the objective of the ideas and methods in this chapter.

Mario was a delightful child. People had been saying so since his birth ten years earlier. He had a sunny personality that always fit in. He was well-liked both by adults and by his peers. He was always part of the group, always "in" on everything. He was a serious-minded boy who had faith in his parents and in people in general.

Then his parents began to see a potentially negative side to Mario's universal acceptance by others. They began to realize that one of the main reasons he was always with the crowd was because he always went along with the crowd. Recently a group of boys had tortured a cat, swinging it by its tail, throwing it in water, pulling its ears, even tying a firecracker to its tail and injuring it seriously. Mario, whose sensitive and compassionate nature must have been repulsed by all this, went along with it anyway, presumably to preserve his place as part of the group. He had made other bad choices for similar reasons.

His parents, Manuel and Maria, knew that somehow they had to change the pattern. After some serious thought and discussion, Manuel and Maria arranged to take Mario—just Mario—to a nice restaurant for a special dinner. Their topic of discussion was decisions.

They started by telling Mario that there are two kinds of decisions. One kind should be easy because it is a choice between a right and a wrong thing, and we usually know which is right. The second kind involves lots of options, and different ones are right for different people.

Mario seemed to understand the distinction. They discussed examples of the first kind: whether we should steal, whether we should lie, whether we should be kind, whether we should hurt people (or animals). They discussed examples of the second kind: what classes to take in school, which activities to get involved in, whom to marry, what job to have, where to live.

Then his parents asked Mario when he thought was the best time to make each kind of decision. After some discussion, they arrived at the right answer together. Decisions of the first kind should be made now, *in advance*, because we already know the right answers and we shouldn't wait until we are in difficult situations before we commit ourselves. Decisions of the second kind must wait until we actually face them, and then we try to decide thoughtfully and correctly.

They talked about examples and situations. "Let's say, Mario, that in a couple of years you are with your buddies, and they decide it would be fun to sniff some glue or try some drugs. They are all doing it and saying how good it makes them feel, and they urge you to try it. When you hesitate they say, 'Come on, Mario, don't be chicken. It won't hurt you—no one will know.' If you haven't made your decision in advance, that might be a tough situation, but if you've already decided never to use drugs, it would be much easier, wouldn't it?"

The dinner meeting went on much longer than anyone had planned. But it was wonderful. Because Mario was treated like an adult, he responded like one. He enjoyed receiving so much attention from both parents, and his attention span seemed longer than they had remembered it.

The result of the discussion was a list, written in Mario's own hand, of all the decisions he was prepared to make right now, the things he could commit to himself and to his parents because he knew they were right. The list included setting a good example for his brother, never using drugs, never doing anything cruel to a person or an animal, telling the truth, never stealing, and never cheating.

As each item was added to Mario's list, he and his parents discussed situations in which holding to the decision would be difficult and temptation would be great. Mario recommitted himself in light of each of these imagined situations. When the list was finished, he dated and signed it. He put it on the door of his closet where he would see it often and would remember that those decisions were already made.

Before they left the restaurant, they also talked about the second kind of decisions. Manuel and Maria told Mario of times in their lives when they had had important decisions to make and how they had thought very carefully about those decisions. They talked about decisions Mario would have to make, and Mario began to understand how to make them.

When the evening was over, the foundation was laid, the trust level built, and the communication channels opened to permit future discussions about individual decisions that would arise. More importantly, Mario came away stronger, more aware of his responsibility to himself and of his control over his own destiny.

B. Methods

1. *Approaches to help small children define "decisions."* (To make the terms *choice* and *decisions* familiar to young children so the words and concepts can be used in later methods.)

(a) *Questions and discussion.* Ask: What is a decision? What does it mean to make a decision? (When you choose or decide for yourself which thing you want or what you want to do.)

Have you made any decisions lately? Stimulate children's thinking by asking, Did you choose what to wear today? Did you choose where to sit on the sofa? Did you decide which book to look at when you first went to school? Did you decide last night whether to watch television or to play with your toys? Did you decide last night to sleep with your teddy bear, or to have the door opened or closed?

Do you like to make decisions?

Do you ever make a wrong decision and wish you could change it? (Everyone does at one time or another. Sometimes we can change a decision and sometimes we can't. When we have an important decision to make, we should think about it first and try to make a good decision that will make us happy.)

(b) *Puppet shows.* (To help small children better understand what decisions are and to help them differentiate between decisions governed by laws or rules and decisions that have to be individually made.)

Using hand puppets, and a little imagination, put on short puppet shows. Use the suggestions listed below or make up some of your own. The characters for the suggested skits are a mother, a father, two girls, and two boys. Any hand puppets will do as long as you identify who is who before each skit.

For a puppet stage, use the back of a sofa or large chair. Kneel behind it or behind a blanket stretched between the backs of two kitchen chairs. The children will be able to see your face, but tell them to pretend that they can't see you. (You should be able to watch them so that you can respond to their reactions.) You will talk for all the characters (one on each hand) and also make necessary explanations as you go along. The puppet who is speaking should be moving while the other one is still, so that the children may follow the story with ease.

Don't worry about your dramatic ability. No matter how amateurish the show is, the children will probably love it and will give their rapt attention. There should be two parts to each show. The first part should involve an unhappy ending, when a puppet child disobeys a rule or makes a bad decision. Then the same situation is repeated with a happy ending as the child obeys the rule or makes a good decision. Each show should be short. You can dramatize three or four situations (each with both endings) in about ten minutes. Discuss the decisions after each show.

Puppet Show 1

Characters needed: Three puppets—a mother and two girls.

The situation: A girl wants to wear her new dress instead of her long pants to school, though the weather is very cold. She discovers that her long tights, which she usually wears with a dress, are in the laundry.

First ending: She decides to wear the dress anyway, without her long tights. She is happy when her best friend compliments her on her pretty dress, but when they go outside to play, her legs are so cold that she must return to the building and cannot play with the other children. She realizes that she has made a bad decision.

Second ending: She decides to wear her long pants and to save the dress to wear on a warmer day. When the children go out to play, she is able to go with them. She realizes that she has made a good decision.

Puppet Show 2

Characters needed: Two puppets—a girl and a mother.

The situation: A girl finds a book of matches on the sidewalk. She knows the rule that she must never play with matches.

First ending: She decides to strike one of the matches. She is delighted that it works, and she becomes so interested in watching it burn that she doesn't blow it out in time, and her fingers are burned. She runs home to her mother, who treats the burns and comforts her. Her mother is disappointed that she broke the rule, but she doesn't punish the little girl; she explains that the girl has already been punished by being burned.

Second ending: The girl decides to take the matches home to her mother. Her mother praises her for obeying the rule.

Puppet Show 3

Characters needed: Three puppets—a mother, a father, and a boy.

The situation: A boy is told that his father is coming home from work early to take him to the circus. His mother says that he must clean his room before he can go.

First ending: He decides to watch just one more cartoon on television before cleaning his room, but he gets interested in television and forgets about it. When his father comes home, the boy's room isn't cleaned up, and by the time the boy finishes the job, they arrive at the circus late and miss the first act. He realizes he has made a bad decision to watch television first and then do his chores.

Second ending: He cleans his room up and then watches television. He realizes he has made a good decision, for he is ready to go to the circus when his father arrives to take him.

Puppet Show 4

Characters needed: Three puppets—two boys and a father.

The situation: A boy is walking home from school with a friend who asks him to come to his house to play for a while. He knows there is a family rule that he should go straight home from school and ask his parents for permission to go to a friend's home. His friend says, "You can call your mother on our phone."

First ending: He goes to his friend's home to call his parents, but the line is busy. Then he becomes interested in his friend's new game and forgets about calling home. About an hour later he suddenly remembers. He knows that he has broken a family rule, and so he hurries home. His parents are upset and tell him that they have been worried about him. They love him very much, but they must discipline him to help him remember to obey the rule. He is not allowed to have his friend over to his house, or to go to his friend's house, for a week.

Second ending: The little boy says, "I'll go home first and ask my parents if I can come to your house. Then, if I can, I'll be right back." His parents give him permission and praise him for remembering and obeying the rule.

2. *Good decision reinforcement.* (Ways to give enough praise and reinforcement for good decisions to *overbalance* the rebuttal and ridicule that may come from the "crowd" who want your child to make the wrong decision.)

(a) *Ancestor stories.* Locate true stories about your own ancestors who had the courage to go against the crowd, to do what they believed was right. Tell the experiences in a way that truly honors that courage and shows how much it pays off in the long run. Relate each ancestor to the child, telling him, "You are this man's great-grandson; the same kind of courage to do right that was in him is in you too."

(b) *Individual attention reinforcement.* In your "weekly sessions" with your children (see chapters 5 and 9), spend some time talking about good choices they have already made. If they have prepared a list of decisions made in advance as suggested in the illustration at the beginning of this chapter, regularly go through that list with them individually. Ask whether the anticipated situations have come up, and praise every incident where they adhered to their decision.

3. *Allowing natural consequences.* (The "innoculation principle"—to help children understand the cause-and-effect nature of their choices while they are young, before their decisions are weighty and the consequences serious enough to have adverse effects on their lives.)

The medical principle of innoculation operates on the premise that a small number of germs can threaten the body just enough to stimulate the production of antibodies. Likewise, small, relatively unimportant bad choices, with their attendant consequences, go further in teaching children to make good decisions than any amount of counsel, advice, or artificial punishment.

Examples of poor choices and possible consequences might include the following:

Failure to practice a piano piece—embarrassment at the recital.

Wearing heavy clothing on a hot day—discomfort and irritation.

Watching a late television show on Friday—missing a family outing early Saturday morning.

Failure to study for a spelling test—a low or failing grade.

There will be many situations in which you will have a clear choice between pushing your child to make the correct choice and letting him choose wrongly and suffer the consequences. The key is to be wise enough to let relatively unimportant choices, especially the ones with rather immediate and noticeable consequences, take their natural course.

When you do allow the child wrong choices, be sure to discuss what happened and why it happened while it is still fresh in his mind. Always go from the specifics of what has just happened to the general principle that wrong decisions almost always catch up with us, whereas good choices in the long run make us happy.

4. *Approaches relating to choice of friends.* (Hardly any subject concerns or occupies conscientious parents so much as their children's choice of associates and friends. It is sometimes easy to overreact, at other times easy to underreact. What is needed is a careful mixture of the two approaches that follow.)

(a) *Engineering good friendships.* If you are aware of a particular child who has some qualities that you feel would be good for your child to acquire, don't be afraid to "engineer" a little matchmaking. Most children under ten or eleven will become friends almost as a matter of course once they are brought together for a period of time. Call the child's parents and compliment them on the qualities you like in their child; they'll appreciate your comments. Then invite their child over for an afternoon, or take him on an outing with your family, or whatever. If you bring the children together in a relaxed atmosphere a couple of times, chances are a friendship will start.

(b) *Building up instead of tearing down.* Too often, when one of our children associates with another child whom we consider to be a negative influence, our first and only thought is to break up the friendship, to separate our child from the source of negative influence. In some cases this may be the appropriate—perhaps the only—thing to do. At other times, however, with a little thought, we could create a situation in which our child helps or influences the other child to change.

Sometimes the process is simple. You may want to initiate a conversation such as the following: "Son, you know, Mike seems like a nice boy, but I was wondering if he does anything that he shouldn't, anything that you wouldn't do."

"Yes, he swears a lot."

"That's too bad. I wonder why he does that."

"I think his dad and mom do."

"Well, you two are pretty good friends, aren't you?"

"Yes."

"Do you think that if he's around you a lot and never hears you swear, he might not do it so much himself?"

"Maybe."

"I think he might not. You might even tell him that you think he should try not to swear. Tell him you like him a lot, but that he doesn't sound good when he swears."

The idea, of course, is to help your child develop leadership qualities and an ability that makes him more likely to influence and change others for good than to yield to a negative influence.

The major problems children have in elementary school often concern friends, not academics. And they are problems that, if not resolved, can affect their self-image into adulthood.

When children are small, their tastes are indiscriminating. As they grow older, they begin to get very definite ideas about certain things. Often the girls eliminate boys from their list of friends, and vice versa. Friends who have similar interests become important, and children begin to appreciate what a real friend is.

Parents are inclined to feel that friends at this age are not terribly important. But friends are important for everyone, regardless of age.

Because each child is so different, and no blanket statement can apply in all cases, we must teach children the basic principles of making friends and let them apply them in their own way. We should talk about friendship and give them some guidance. Too many children are left alone to sort these things out for themselves. If they are having problems with friends at school, they are usually reluctant to talk about them. Their frustrations often manifest themselves in anger and letting off steam at home for seemingly inexplicable reasons.

We can't emphasize strongly enough the need to talk to children about their friends and to teach them how to make friends and how to influence them for good. Children are capable of understanding that making friends is an art.

C. Family Focal Points: Advance Decisions, Family Decisions, Setting an Example

About the time that our children turn nine or ten, we work with them on a list of advance decisions like that described in the illustration for this chapter. As Mario did, they imagined the hardest conceivable situation, decided how they would handle it, and then committed to standing by their decision. The lists are saved in a prominent place and are left "open-ended" so that other advance decisions may be added as the need arises.

Parents can usually prepare their own lists of advance decisions, which can then be used as examples. We also have a list of *family* advance decisions that we have made together—decisions we have decided upon unanimously and absolutely. These include always being totally honest with each other and always supporting one another's interests and activities.

When major family decisions must be made that fall outside of our advance-decision list, we make them together, in a family meeting, following the same procedure we hope the children will learn to follow in their individual decisions. First, we analyze and discuss every aspect, every pro and con, every consequence we can think of. Second, we come to our own best decision, discussing it until it is unanimous. Third, we analyze how we feel about the decision. Do we feel good about it? If not, we start over.

Because we have maintained two separate homes for the past several years and moved back and forth between them (as well as to England for three years), our children have made a rather wide variety of acquaintances and friends. We have been delighted at their opportunities to know children from many cultures, races, and differing situations. We have tried to cultivate in our children a "contribution perspective" that essentially says, "I am fortunate to come from a close-knit family. I am no better than other children, but I do have a responsibility to set an example."

As with teaching most forms of responsibility, the real key is in setting a good example, creating an understanding of the principles involved, and developing ways of consistent follow-up so that children are always aware of choices and have ability to weigh them carefully.

Responsibility for Character 8

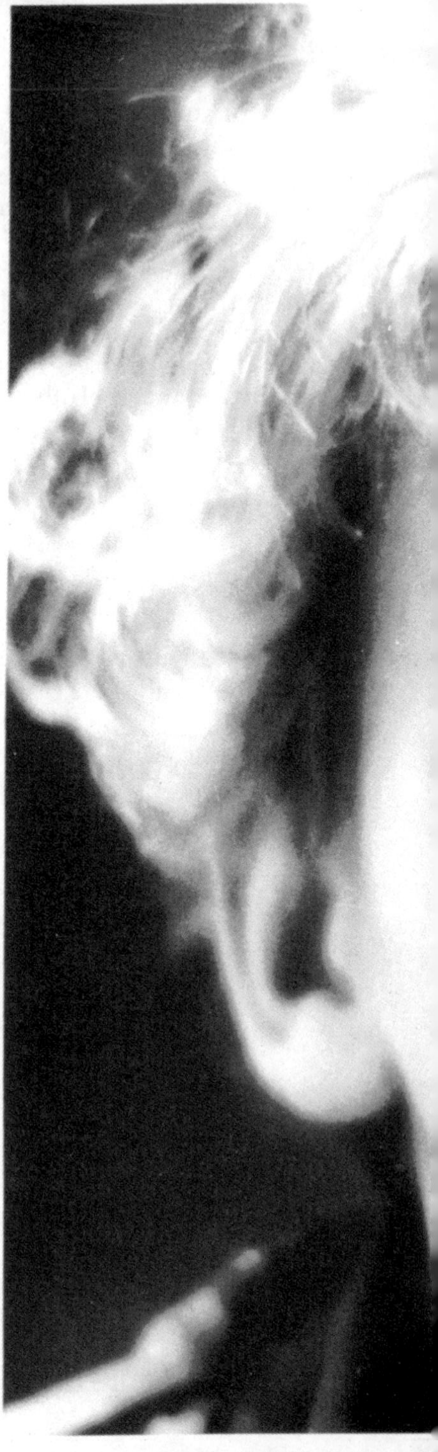

It has been said that, by the time he is fifty, every person has the face he deserves. The same thing could be said of character, only at a much earlier age.

A. Definition and Illustration

It has been said that if we sow a thought, we reap an action; sow an action, reap a habit; sow a habit, reap a character. One of the intriguing things about this statement is the relationship between habit and character. This chapter will help you foster the kinds of habits and procedures in your home that help children to develop strong characters, and to realize that the characters they build are not something inherited but something developed, something for which they are responsible.

"Now, there is a boy with real character," Jim Bullip said to himself as he picked up his morning paper out of the newly fallen snow on the porch and watched the paperboy ride away on his bicycle into the predawn blackness.

Jim, unable to sleep that morning, had come downstairs to read before his wife or children awoke. He walked back into the warm kitchen thinking about the paperboy. "That boy has character." But just what did he mean by that? Why had that word come to mind? Jim had met the paperboy just a few days before when he came around to collect the monthly subscription fee, and he had liked him instantly. The boy had an open smile and looked him straight in the eye. He didn't seem to mind being out collecting bills while most of the other boys his age were playing basketball after school or watching television at home. Jim knew that the boy's mother was a widow, that they had little money, and that the paper route was only one of two or three jobs the boy held down to help support his mother and four younger sisters.

The boy was probably only a grade or two ahead of Jim's oldest son, Teddy, who was in the fifth grade. Yet he seemed much older than Teddy. Somehow he had more *character*.

Was life too soft for Teddy and the other children? Had Jim and Belva been so anxious to give them everything that there were no opportunities for them to struggle and grow? A quotation from somewhere came into Jim's mind: "Parents who do too much *for* their children will find they can't do much *with* them."

For the next few days, Jim was especially observant of his children, particularly of Teddy and Jayne, the two oldest. They had a few pressures from school and some household responsibilities that Belva had given them, but not much more than that. Their lives were fairly sheltered, pretty easy. Too easy? Jim wondered.

At Christmastime, Jim's cousin Henry, who ran a large farm in eastern Oregon, came to visit for a day or two. His children were approximately the same ages as Jim and Belva's, so it was natural to do some observing and a little comparing. There it was again—that hard-to-define but easy-to-see something called character. Henry's children had a lot of it. It wasn't outgoingness; it was something else, something that had to do with self-esteem and a sense of usefulness. These children had to work. They had developed the self-discipline of getting out of a warm bed each morning before dawn to go out into the cold and do chores. They probably didn't enjoy it, but the discipline and responsibility of it had produced character. Jim couldn't help associating them with the paperboy.

Between Christmas and New Year's, Jim and Belva talked a lot about developing character in their children. They decided to use the New Year as an excuse to turn over a new leaf. They defined several tasks for which the older children could take responsibility. They decided everyone would get out of bed an hour earlier each morning to allow the children time for music practice. They agreed to require each child, when he turned twelve, to earn his own spending money. They presented these and their other character-building ideas to the children in a well-planned presentation.

Implementation was not quite as easy, but gradually they noticed some changes. Jim decided once again that the best way to describe the changes was the word *character*. The children seemed to have a brighter look, a little more self-esteem, a certain budding sense of independence.

Perhaps the biggest change was not in the children at all, but in Jim and Belva. As Teddy began to respond to some of the increased challenges, his parents found themselves talking to him and thinking of him more as an adult and less as a child. Priorities and values were actually discussed instead of lectured about, and they began to take the time to answer Teddy's questions about sex and other subjects that they had previously avoided or put off.

What makes certain people extraordinary? What differentiates the virtuoso pianist, the convincing actor, the literary giant? What produces a successful teacher or an outstanding mother? While many factors contribute to the character-building process, there is one common thread in the lives of great people that can be singled out and examined: sacrifice!

A friend who is a successful musician and composer once said during a dinner conversation, "While I was still in school, I received large checks in the mail, the royalties from a television show I had scored during a summer vacation. My friends always looked at me with amazement. 'How would it be?' they would say with envy as I deposited them in my ever-growing bank account. What they failed to realize was that while they were out playing football and Frisbee, I was inside at the piano, practicing. Even now people say to me, 'I'd give anything to be able to play like that!' I have to smile. I'd like to say, 'Anything but ten hours a day for twenty years of your life!'"

Natural talent is certainly a part of the lives of many outstanding people, but the real growth in character takes place because of sacrifice.

Each of us can think of sacrifices we have made that have helped us build character. Even our eleven-year-old can now see how the sacrifice of a little sleep in the morning and a lot of television-watching in the evening can allow her to do the kind of practicing that will make her a musician, and the kind of reading that will expand her vision.

We often become so wrapped up trying to give our children everything possible, every opportunity and every advantage, that it is easy to forget that they need to sacrifice. Sometimes it's tempting to do the paper route when Johnny has so much homework, or an important soccer practice. But we must remember the simple fact that sacrifice produces character.

B. Methods

1. *Approaches to building self-esteem in small children.* (To help children develop sufficient self-respect so that they take pride in who and what they are.)

(a) *"Unique You" booklet.* Purchase simple loose-leaf or report binders, one for each child, and construction paper. Let the children create the covers by drawing pictures of themselves and putting their names on with glitter. Then make up the following pages:

Handprints. Using white construction paper and your choice of water-soluble black ink, a black-ink stamp pad, or black tempera paint, have each child make his own handprint. Have him make another handprint on a piece of paper large enough to contain all the children's handprints. Have each child sign his name by his own handprint.

Foods I like. Have on hand, or have children cut from magazines, a generous supply of small pictures of different foods. Have the children choose their favorite foods and paste the pictures on construction paper. As they cut and paste, emphasize the differences: Mary likes macaroni. Jason likes hot dogs. Jenny likes strawberries.

Things I am especially good at. Help the children make up a page listing their "gifts." You may want to refer to some of the gift-identifying methods in chapter 5.

"Favorites" page. Have each child list his favorite color, favorite television show, favorite book, and so forth.

Places I've been. Have each child list places he has visited.

Things I might be when I grow up. Have each child list what he would like to do when he grows up.

Keep the books handy and add other pages or review what is already there when you sense a child's need for a boost of self-identity or self-esteem.

(b) *Story: "Everyone Is Special."*

Once there was a king who ordered all his subjects to wear masks just like his face, and robes just like his. After many days of confusion (because no one was able to tell one person from another), the queen said, "You may be king, but you have a lot to learn." She explained that people look and act different for a reason.

"What reason?" he asked.

"The best reason in the world," she answered. "If everybody's different, then everybody is special!"

"Do you mean," said the king, "that being the only person who really looks and acts like me makes me special?"

The queen explained that being yourself makes you a *special* person, but you have to work at making yourself the *best* person you can be.

The king decided that he should help people be themselves instead of making rules that they should be someone else. He invited his subjects to come to a party at the castle to celebrate their differences. They all had a great time being themselves. Everybody looked different, and they were glad they did. They were glad to be special.

(c) *Game: "What I Like about You."* Gather the whole family on the carpet and place an empty chair in front of and facing the group. Tell the children, "Each of you is different from anyone else, and each of you is special. There are many things about you that make you special. Let's find out what some of those things are."

Invite one child to sit on the chair in front of the group; then ask the other children to think about that child and what they like about him. Say, "You can each tell ______ what you like about him."

You, the parent, take the first turn by saying something nice about the child, such as, "I like the way Ben shares with everyone," "I think Jessica has a pretty singing voice," "Chris is good at doing puzzles," "Amy has such lovely brown eyes," "Daddy is always smiling," and so forth. Add several compliments to the ones that the children mention. Help each child to feel special. Be sure that you are sincere in the things you say. Be prepared ahead of time with some good, true thoughts about each one. This will help you to know and appreciate each child's own special qualities more.

(d) *Discussion.* Talk with the children about how one must like himself in order to like others: "If you don't like yourself, you'll always be wishing you could be like someone else or do what someone else can do, or you'll wish that you had the things they have. Then you'll stop liking yourself and other people." Help them to understand that if they feel good about themselves and the way they look and the things they can do, and if they remember that they are special in their own way, then they won't mind if someone can do something they can't do or has something they don't have, and they can like that person.

Give examples, such as, "if Tom can skip better than you can, you won't mind, because you can throw a ball better than he can," or "If Alice has a new doll and you don't, you won't mind, because you have a new baby brother." Tell them, "If you're happy with the things you have and the things you can do, you will like yourself. Then you'll notice the special things about other people, and you'll like them too."

(e) *The meaning of "unique."* Tell the children that you are going to teach them a new word. "The word is *unique*. Can you say that? Say it again. Does anyone know what the word means?"

Explain that *unique* means "one of a kind." If something is unique, there is nothing else exactly like it. Give some examples such as each snowflake, each tree, each kitten. They may be almost alike, but not exactly alike. Something about them is different.

Is there anyone else in the whole world who is *exactly* like you?" (No.) "Then *you* are unique. Let me hear you say, 'I am unique.'" (I am unique.) "What does that mean?" (It means no one else is exactly like me.)

Then tell the children that is what makes them so special and so important. "You are the only one just like you."

2. *Discussion of "character."* (To help children understand "character" and its importance and to prepare them for some of the other methods that follow.)

Build a discussion around the following points:

Remember when we discussed *gifts* and *talents*? (Yes.)

What are some of the gifts each of you has? (The children give examples.)

Do all people have the same gifts? (No. The children give examples.)

Are some people better at some things and others better at other things? (Yes. The children give examples.)

Tonight we are going to talk about a different kind of thing called "character." Character is something *everyone* can have, no matter what his gifts are. Can you think of anything that works like that? (Honesty, obedience, courtesy, dependability, helpfulness, and so forth.)

All those things are part of character. The more of them that you have, the better your character is. Character is the kind of person you really are, deep inside. Now, if you don't have some of these character things, can you get them? (Yes.)

How? (By making up your mind to have them and working to do so.)

Can anyone help you get them? (Yes—your parents, your brothers and sisters, friends.)

Can these people help you if you don't want to have these things? (Not much.)

You might want to make up your own family's list of what

character includes and put it up where it is visible during the month you are concentrating on responsibility for character.

3. *Building self-image in children.* (To ingrain into children's minds the self-image of a strong and positive character.)

Because of children's strong proclivity to become precisely what they believe you think they are, this method becomes particularly important. It also requires significant mental effort on your part.

Write out a description of the basic character of each child. Be honest in your assessments but be very positive. Start with the strongest character qualities you have observed in him (courage to try new things, honesty, sensitivity, concern for younger children, and so forth). Then proceed to areas where you think he has good *potential.* (Perhaps he shows signs of being a good, steady worker or of being especially dependable.)

Remember that you are looking for *character* traits, not skills or talents. It is hard mental work to carefully analyze the character qualities of each child, but it is also rewarding and enjoyable, particularly if you can do it together as a couple.

After you have itemized both the strongest and potentially strong traits of a child, go on to his weaknesses, but state them positively (such as, Jimmy is working hard at being more tidy; he is trying to gain better control of his temper, and so forth.)

Type or print the completed descriptions (no more than one page per child) and read them through with the children, either all together as a family or individually with each child. Tell the children that you are so proud of each of them and of their character that you wanted to write it all down. Give each child a copy of your character description of them. Keep your own copies in a safe place; read through them periodically, and, as a child improves in an area, change the description from "he's trying hard to . . ." to "he is very good at . . ." Share them with the children regularly.

4. *Family character.* (To help children feel the healthy pride of being part of a family that is collectively committed to certain character traits.)

As you concentrate in your family on the qualities of character, you will realize that excellence in some of those qualities is within your grasp. For example, if you and each child old enough to understand never steal anything from the store, then you are excellent in that area.

Ask the children if there are some things you excel in as a family, such as not stealing, not cheating at school, always trying your hardest. Make a list. Ask, "What are some things we ought to excel at but we sometimes aren't?" (Telling the truth, keeping the family laws, minding our parents, and so forth.) Then pick out one of those things that you all think you can excel at. Put it on a list in pencil and tell the children you will go over it again with pen when the whole family excels at it.

As you make this list visible and talk about it regularly, a kind of family character and code of behavior will emerge. From it, the children will draw strength and commitment for their own developing characters.

5. *Character through tradition and heritage.* (To help children feel a sense of pride in who they are and an accompanying form of self-responsibility.)

(a) *Ancestor stories.* (See chapter 5.) Locate any stories about your parents or grandparents that illustrate good character traits. Talk about how the potential for strong character is often inherited, but how it must still be worked at and developed.

(b) *Character-building family traditions.* Most families have traditions they are not even aware of, things they do somewhat regularly on holidays or birthdays or during certain seasons of the year. Write the character-building traditions down on a calendar, according to which month they occur in. As children anticipate these traditions, a character-molding influence is exerted. Such influences *institutionalize* a family and give children a certain security or identity that strengthens their character and helps them to stand firm in their own beliefs even when they are faced with peers who believe and act differently.

Some personal examples of family traditions appear in this chapter's "family focal points."

The existence of positive traditions and family- and ancestor-oriented identity puts a child in a strong character mold and makes it possible for a parent to remind him of a lot of character-related things simply by saying, "Remember who you are!"

6. *Sacrifice.* (To help children learn the meaning of the word and feel its effects.)

(a) *Discussion.* Talk about the word *sacrifice.* What does it mean? Is it good? Explain that the best definition of sacrifice is

"Giving up something good in order to have something better." Think of and discuss examples, such as giving up a Saturday morning to help a widow by mowing her lawn, resulting in a feeling of satisfaction; giving up a special toy to a poor child in order to make him happy as well as make you happy inside.

(b) *Anonymous toy gift.* Children can learn a great deal about sacrifice by picking one of their nice toys, wrapping it, and leaving it anonymously for a less-fortunate child. Afterward, use your imagination and help your child envision the other child and how happy the gift has made him.

Children develop real character when they realize that they have a responsibility to themselves to rise above their negative feelings. It comes when they discipline themselves to do something they don't really want to do, simply because they know it is right. It ranges from being happy for rather than jealous of a sister's good fortune, to doing homework and practicing without being told. It is strengthened every time the ten-year-old boy voluntarily shovels the snow from the elderly man's walk next door or a big sister takes the baby to play when she sees her tired mother's need for help.

I recently visited a friend's home and noticed five or six bud vases in the kitchen cupboard. Each contained a dead rose. After a few minutes of small talk, I decided to ask why she was keeping the dead roses.

"Oh, I just can't bear to throw them away," she explained. "They are gifts from Kristen's friends. They were all in the same ballet class and all tried out for a part in *The Nutcracker.* Even though each wanted the part desperately, when Kristen won the audition, each of these friends showed her true character and good wishes with a rose." What wise parents behind those lovely children!

Children can do remarkably mature things when we take the time to help them understand how much their actions affect others, and how important it is for them to be responsible to themselves for their own character.

C. Family Focal Points: Character-Building Family Traditions, Early Morning Practice, Personal Standards Discussions

For many years we have sponsored a Chilean child through a foster parents' program. Her picture hangs on the wall. One evening while we were living in England, we were in the family room, which was separated from the living room by some French doors. It was dark in the living room, and the children remarked that the glass in the French doors was like a mirror—they could see their own images in it.

Then someone turned on the living-room light, the "mirrors" became "windows," and instead of their own reflections, they saw the little Chilean girl's picture. The result was an interesting discussion with the older children about turning the mirrors of our lives into windows, seeing the needs of others instead of our own, and being part of the solution rather than part of the problem. Our little Chilean child has become a symbol of sacrifice. The children want to give of their means to help her. At Christmas one of them volunteered her piggy bank and regularly collected donations for Christmas gifts for needy children from other members of the family.

Helping the needy can become a pattern in a family. Patterns are essentially traditions—things we do regularly, look forward to, and feel secure through. Family traditions help children build character in at least two ways: (1) Traditions themselves can be related to unselfishness, to sacrifices, to improvement. (2) The mere existence of traditions institutionalizes a family, gives children a feeling of belonging and of security in being part of something bigger than themselves. This security is what gives them the inner courage that is a major part of character and of living what they believe.

Entire books have been written on family traditions. We think the best traditions are those that build character, that you have developed yourself, and in some cases that are traditions established by earlier generations of your family.

We try to formalize our traditions. In the same book where we have our ancestor stories (see chapters 3 and 5), we list our traditions by month. Each tradition is illustrated by a picture drawn by one of the children. There are at least two traditions for each month, though some months, like December, have many more. A few examples are:

(a) January—Josh's birthday. We build a huge snowman in the backyard and invite neighbors over to see it and to have birthday cake.

Shawni's birthday. On the nearest Friday when there is a nearly full or full moon, we get up in the middle of the night and go on a mystical moonlit hike in the snow.

(b) February—valentines. For each of our children, we try to think of one person who probably isn't getting any valentines, perhaps a widow or shut-in. The child makes a special one for that person.

(c) August—Saydi's birthday. In the evening we put her birthday cake in a big pan, light the candles, and float the pan in the lake. When the waves finally carry it in to shore we eat the cake on the beach.

(d) November—Thanksgiving cards. We send these instead of Christmas cards. Each child writes a short poem on gratitude and friendship.

(e) December—a neighborhood concert. Our children and others from the neighborhood perform for parents, who pay a rather large admittance fee for seats at the concert. The children all sign a letter to send with the money to needy children.

(f) Quarterly book review. Every three months each family member reports on the best things he has read that quarter.

Self-control and physical self-discipline have a lot to do with character. Difficult as it is, during the school year we get up with the children every weekday morning at 6:30 for music practice. In our case, Mom is the teacher and Dad practices cello while the other children practice their own instruments. Twice a week we combine to play ensemble music together. In addition to the music, each child has a household job to do before school.

One of the most important areas of physical self-discipline is that of sex. We think that this is something that should be discussed in the family, and that it should be an important part of a child's orientation as soon as he is old enough to understand, generally around the age of eight. Sometime within the first month after his eighth birthday, we have an individual and special talk with the child about the "facts of life." Some say this is too early and that children only eight years old are neither interested in nor capable of understanding the facts of life. We have found the contrary. They are both interested and capable of understanding. If you put off this discussion, your children will probably hear their first talk of sex from peers rather than from you.

We try to make the discussion special in several ways:

1. *Anticipation.* We start telling them, even before their

birthday that we are soon going to tell them about one of the most wonderful and beautiful things in the world.

2. *Atmosphere.* We arrange for the child to stay up later than usual so that he is the only one up with us. Then we either have some refreshments or build a fire in the fireplace to add to the special feeling.

3. *Positive orientation.* The whole discussion is upbeat and positive. The cautions and warnings can come later.

There are two or three good, tastefully illustrated books written to help children understand reproductive facts. We picked our favorite based on its positive, love-and-commitment approach. We let the discussion take as much time as necessary. We try to draw out the child's comments throughout, and we concentrate on three things: (a) how beautiful and wonderful the process is (both sex and the growth of a baby); (b) how great it will be when he is old enough to be married and have children—and how happy we will be to be grandparents; and (c) how the whole thing is so special that it should be shared only with the one special person he or she is married to.

Some children show more interest initially than others, but this first, major discussion opens the way for communication, makes it easier for questions to be asked as they arise, and sets the stage for further, in-depth discussions that ought to be held every year or so.

Responsibility for Potential 9

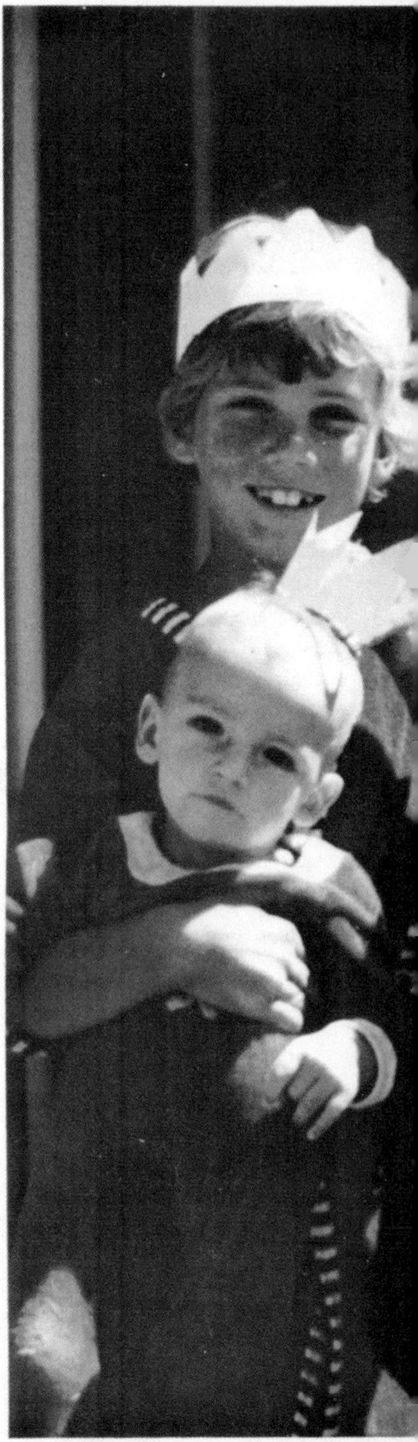

The potential of every child is unimaginable, yet, by trying *to imagine it, we can help that child reach toward it.*

A. Definition and Illustration

There are two levels of responsibility. On one level, being responsible means not doing irresponsible things. On a higher level, it means doing all that one can do, becoming all that one can become, developing all that one has.

The highest form of self-discipline is reaching—reaching for the best that is in us, and sometimes even reaching for more than is in us.

A person who achieves and succeeds, both within himself and within his world, undergoes a certain transition at an early point in his life. He changes from an ordinary, average person, reacting to life as it comes day by day, into a person who designs his own destiny, who comprehends the control he has over his own life, who decides to step out, to lead, to become what he is intended to be and to do his best in all areas.

The objective of this chapter is to help our children begin to make that transition.

When Larry was about nine and a half, he became best friends with Peter, a new next-door neighbor who was a year older than Larry. It was an unfortunate friendship, at least to begin with.

Peter was a particularly lazy boy whose only objective was to escape responsibility and learning of any kind with the least amount of friction possible. He missed school whenever he could find an excuse, and he did poorly when he was there. He was sloppy in his dress and his language. He had no hobbies or intellectual interests. His only interest was in baseball. He collected baseball cards. He watched every televised baseball game, and he played everywhere and anywhere he could—even by himself, bouncing a ball off a wall, when he couldn't find anyone else to play with.

In this new friendship, Larry's own already substantial interest in baseball doubled, and his efforts at such things as school, music lessons, and tidiness were greatly reduced. Barbara and Benson Letterman, Larry's parents, were at a loss to know what to do. There was no support from Peter's parents, and the whole situation had developed so fast that they had done little to stop it.

Their first approach at redirecting Larry's attention was a total failure. It was a lecture on how unimportant baseball is compared to studies, books, college, work, and success. Larry responded by telling them that Reggie Jackson made more in a week than they did in a year.

Barbara and Benson retreated, retrenched, and planned their next move. Maybe baseball wasn't the enemy after all; perhaps it was the key to teaching lessons about ability, about goal-striving and potential-reaching, about doing your best—the kind of lessons that could open the door to other things.

The next week they invited Peter over for dinner. After a nice general chat, the discussion took the following direction: "You boys have some real potential in baseball. We've watched you. But your Little League team has won only two games so far. Let's figure out some ways in which you two can improve your own games so that the team can start winning. Let's have a little batting practice starting tonight."

In the days ahead, Benson and Barbara helped both boys set some specific goals: how many hits per game, how many strikeouts (for Peter, who was the pitcher), how few walks, how few errors, and so forth. They wrote the goals down and helped the boys create a plan for how to reach them, including how many hours of practice would be needed each night and what kind of practice would produce the necessary results. Benson set aside the time necessary to help, but he only assisted with the boys' goals—the initiative was always theirs. They set up a chart with a check-off system for their practice and circles to be filled in after each game if they reached their goals.

They didn't talk much about schoolwork or music practice or other things for a week or two, and unfortunately, the results showed it. But the boys did get better at baseball. They began to reach their personal goals each week. They now liked the game even more than before, because in addition to the fun of baseball itself, they had the satisfaction of reaching personal goals.

It was time for phase two of the Lettermans' plan. They sat down with Larry after dinner one night and talked about how enjoyable it is to set goals and to work toward and reach them.

Baseball, of course, was the example and talking point. Then they asked Larry if he would like to set some goals in other areas as well, not in place of the baseball goals, but along with them. Much to their relief, it worked.

"Yeah," said Larry. "I'm getting tired of doing nothing but baseball."

In the discussion that followed, everyone agreed that baseball is wonderful, but it is not everything. They also agreed that Peter was a good friend for Larry, but that he was too wrapped up in baseball and allowed other aspects of his life to suffer. They talked too about what a good idea it is to have goals in several areas so you'll see what you're good at, so that if you get discouraged or disappointed in one area, you can still take pride and do well in another.

The moment was complete when Larry suggested that if he did well in other things, maybe Peter would notice and want to do some of those things himself.

As the Lettermans went to bed that night, they realized that their discussion with Larry—probably a turning point and starting point for the rest of his life—would never have happened if they'd tried to go around baseball and Peter rather than using both of them to teach Larry.

Two mistakes are common in teaching children responsibility for their potential. One is neglecting to expose them to the wondrous possibilities open to them because of their interests and aptitudes. The other is to expose them to so many things that they become overcommitted and have to sacrifice their responsibilities to their families and others.

In one neighborhood where we lived, many of the children seemed so overwhelmed with piano, violin, swimming, and skiing lessons, choir practice, and Boy Scout badges that they had no time for other responsibilities. Their mothers spent most of their time taking them to and from lessons; they also felt so sorry for their busy, overworked children that they were cleaning their rooms for them. They did not dare ask an older child to care for a baby brother, because the older child was so busy "reaching his potential."

In our opinion, either of these two mistakes is as bad as the other.

B. Methods

1. *Approaches to help small children understand setting and reaching objectives.*

(a) Story: "Sam and the Circus Money." Sam was watching television. Between two shows was a commercial about the circus. On the screen were elephants and dancing bears and clowns. A voice said, "The circus is coming to your town! Don't miss it!"

Sam ran to tell his mother he couldn't miss the circus. His mother said, "Sam, we've just spent a lot of money on your birthday. If you want to go to that circus, you'll have to earn enough money to buy your own ticket."

Sam thought hard about that—so hard that he didn't even watch the rest of the television show. He looked under all the cushions on the couch and chairs and found two dimes. He asked his mother how much a ticket cost. She said, "Two dollars." "How many dimes is that?" asked Sam. "Twenty," said his mother. "As many as all of your fingers and all of your toes." "I've got two already," Sam said, holding up his dimes. His mother smiled at him and took his hand. "Come with me," she said.

Sam's mother got a large sheet of paper and drew a king-size "20" on it. Then she made a long tube by the side with some marks on it. The paper looked like this:

She colored in two squares in the tube with a red crayon, like this:

Sam got the idea even before she told him. He said, "Every time I get another dime, I'll color a square until I get up to 20!" "Right," said his mother, "and there are some old soda bottles in the basement that are worth ten cents each."

Sam found three bottles in the basement. He put them in his wagon and pulled them around the corner to the grocery store, where he got three dimes. He colored in three more squares.

"What now, Mom?" Sam asked.

"Can you think of any more ways to earn some more dimes?" she responded.

Sam said, "More soda bottles."

His mother replied, "Sorry, that's all we've got."

Sam said, "Maybe Mr. Johnson next door has some. I'll go see." Mr. Johnson didn't have any old soda bottles, but he did have a backyard that needed cleaning, and he told Sam he would give him two dimes to do it. Sam did it.

Sam kept thinking of things to do. By the end of the week, do you know what his chart looked like? That's right, it was completely filled in—and it was a very good circus!

On the way home from the circus, Sam, who had been thinking hard, said, "Mom, do you think I could ever earn enough money to buy myself a two-wheeled bike?" "I think so," said his mother, "but it would take a long time."

That night his parents had a long talk—and got a good idea. The next morning Sam's father said, "Sam I think if you were to raise some tomatoes in the garden this year, you could earn enough to buy a bike. Let's use two dollars of my money to buy some tomato plants. If you take good care of them and sell the tomatoes when they grow, you can get enough money to give me back my two dollars and to buy your own bike."

All summer Sam watered his plants and pulled weeds. When the tomatoes got red, he picked them and put them in a bucket; then he knocked on the neighbors' doors. "Would you like to buy some tomatoes?" he said. "Only a nickel each." Every day more tomatoes were red. Every day Sam sold them. By autumn Sam had sold all the tomatoes. He had enough money to pay his father the two dollars and also to buy one present for himself: a red bike, the same color as those tomatoes.

(b) *Story: "Betsy's Goal."* In your own words tell the following story about Betsy, who was looking forward to her birthday the next month and the party she was going to invite all her friends to.

When Betsy's father came home from work, he said he had been transferred in his job, and they would have to move to another town in just one week. Betsy felt very sad, because they would be moving before her birthday, and she wouldn't know anyone in her new school. Whom could she invite to her party? Her mother told her that perhaps she could have a goal of making some new friends in time for her birthday party. Betsy decided she would do just that. She decided she wanted to invite ten friends.

The first day in the new town Betsy met a boy her own age while she was waiting for the school bus. "Hi! I'm Betsy," she said. "I just moved here." The little boy was friendly with her. Then she said the same thing to a girl on the bus. By the time she got to school, she already had *two* new friends.

The next day she noticed a boy in the school yard who looked lonely, and she asked him to play on the teeter-totter with her. They became friends, so now she had *three* friends.

The next day she helped a girl tie her shoe. *Four* friends.

The next day it rained, and she shared her umbrella with two children waiting for the bus. *Six* friends.

That evening her grandmother came to visit and brought Betsy a bag of peanuts, which she decided to save and share at school. At recess she shared with several children. She now had *ten* new friends. She invited them all to come to her birthday party on Saturday.

On Saturday morning Betsy decorated the living room with paper streamers and flowers, and she had a wonderful, happy party with all her new friends.

Ask, What was Betsy's goal? (To make some new friends before her birthday.) Did she reach her goal? How long did it take? How did she do it?

Make sure the children understand that Betsy set a goal—decided what she wanted to do, planned how to do it, and worked hard to reach her goal. Ask, Do you think she was happy when she reached her goal?

(c) *Your goal, their goal.* Tell the children that *you* have a goal. Have one in mind to tell them about. It should be something they can see you working on and something they can see the results of.

Some suggestions are: lose five pounds, make some

kitchen curtains, clean the carpets, learn to bake bread. Choose a goal you can reach. Tell the children what you will do and how you plan to reach your goal. Then show them the chart you will use to record your progress as you work on your goal and to show when you have achieved it.

Draw a circle on a piece of paper and divide it into eight pie-shaped wedges. With colored markers, show how you will fill in a portion of the circle (a different color each time) whenever you work on your goal. Then, when you reach your goal, the circle will be all filled in.

Then say, "Would *you* like to set a goal and work on it and have a goal chart to fill in like this? Think about what you might want for a goal—something good that you really want to do."

If the children have ideas about goals right away, let them suggest them. You might make some suggestions also. If they say something like "Learn to ride a bike," say, "That's a good goal, but it will take quite a long time. Let's think of one you can do this week."

Suggested goals for preschoolers might include learning to tie their shoes, learning to zip their coat, learning to write their name, sitting quietly at listening time, never hitting others, learning to do a hard puzzle, learning to skip.

(d) *Puppet shows.* You will need simple hand puppets to represent a boy, a girl, and a mother.

Kneel behind a sofa or large chair and use the back of it as a puppet stage. Each "show" should last only two or three minutes, and you should give explanations of what is happening, where necessary, as well as speak for the characters. The children are better able to follow the story if the character who is speaking moves a little while the other one is held still. Children, with their active imaginations, can easily interpret the movements to be the tying of a shoe, or zipping of a coat, or whatever the dialogue indicates the puppet is doing.

Use the following ideas or make up some of your own that might better fit the goals that your children need.

Puppet Show 1

A boy who will soon be five wants to learn to tie his shoes before he goes to kindergarten. His mother gives him one of his father's old shoes and puts long laces in it. She shows him how to tie the knot, and he practices it over and over until he can do it. Then she shows him how to make the loop and wrap the other lace around and poke it through. This is more difficult, but he keeps trying. Every day he works on his goal until he can finally tie the shoe by himself. He is very happy. He claps his hands and says, "I reached my goal! I reached my goal!" (Of course, you just pretend to have a shoe.)

Puppet Show 2

A little girl sets a goal to learn to zip her own coat. Every morning when it is time to go to kindergarten, she puts on her coat and her mother shows her how to hold her hands on the zipper and put one side into the other. Each time she works on her goal, she can fill in a little of the circle on her goal chart. Then one day she zips her coat up all by herself. Her mother says, "Good for you. Now if you can do it alone just two more times, we can fill in your whole circle." The little girl jumps up and down, claps her hands, and cries, "I reached my goal! I reached my goal!"

Puppet Show 3

A little boy has a hard time sitting quietly at dinner time. He sets a goal to learn to obey that family rule. When it is dinner time, he tries not to bother anyone else. He decides not to sit next to his little brother, so he won't be tempted to play with him. When another child screams or acts noisy at the table, he whispers, "Don't—I'm working on my goal." Each day he gets to fill in a little of his goal chart, and then one day his mother doesn't have to remind him even once to sit still or eat his food, so he can fill in *all* of his circle on his goal chart. He claps his hands and cries, "I reached my goal! I reached my goal!"

(e) *Discussion about all the goals the children have already reached.* Let the children tell you about all the things they could not do when they were just babies but can do now: turn over, pick things up, drink from a cup, crawl, walk, talk, climb, run, sing, feed themselves, dress themselves, use the toilet, paint pictures, help others. Say, "Maybe you didn't know what a goal was, and you didn't have a goal chart for each thing you learned, but you did *practice* and *try* and *work hard* until you learned to do all those things. Each time you learned to do something new, all by yourself, you were very happy."

Ask the children to each think of one thing they could not do earlier but can do now, and to show that to the family by acting it out. Help them to choose things that they can demonstrate. You may have to make specific suggestions to some of the children.

2. *Adaptation of methods from previous chapters.*

(a) *Four-facet review* (see chapter 5). While holding your monthly review, focus on the potential of each of your children in all four areas. What do you foresee for each of them physically, mentally, socially, and emotionally? Think of their potential by comparing what they *are* doing with what you think they *could* do.

In these monthly parent-to-parent sessions, best held privately in a quiet restaurant, you will find that specific ideas for how to stimulate potential will come to you. The goal is not to think of ways to push any facet of a child's development faster than is natural and enjoyable; rather, you are looking for ideas as to how you, as parents, can help each child to further appreciate his potential and to feel responsible for being the best he can be.

(b) *Build self-esteem and individual uniqueness and confidence* (see chapter 8). These ideas are equally important in this chapter, because the more self-esteem children have, the more they will believe it matters what they do and what they become.

(c) *Ancestor stories.* Find any incidents in your or your ancestors' lives that illustrate achieving potential, pulling oneself up by the bootstraps, or other such qualities.

(d) *Reinforcement.* Remember that praising the effort is far better than praising only the result. If you watch for and notice when children really make an effort and go beyond themselves, you can give lavish praise. Reinforce the idea that the strength of the *try* is what counts—in other words, doing one's best.

3. *Consistent scheduling.* (To give children the discipline of doing certain things in a certain order each day, and to illustrate how potential is reached through consistency and perseverance.)

A home is not an army barracks and should not be run like one. It does, however, pay great dividends to have certain things happen on a dependable, consistent, disciplined basis. This helps children not only in achieving potential but also in building character. As far as possible, breakfast and dinner ought to be served at the same time each day, both with all family members present. Responsibilities such as household chores, music practice, and homework should be set in priority so that they are accomplished before other things, such as watching television, are permitted.

With children in elementary school, homework should usually be done before dinner, and certainly before any television watching is permitted.

Fortunately, good habits are as difficult to break as bad ones, and if children develop a pattern of doing a thing at a consistent, predictable time, they will stay with it and greatly increase their chances of reaching their potential in that thing.

4. *Story: "The Drop of Rain That Didn't Fall."* (To help children feel that if they don't do their best, it will affect other people.)

Tell the following story in your own words:

Randy the raindrop was supposed to jump out of his fleecy, little gray cloud and fall down to earth to water a rose. But Randy was lazy. He liked the soft little cloud; he was comfortable there. Besides, what difference would it make if he never fell. He was just one little raindrop.

So Randy didn't do his job. He didn't do his best. He didn't fall. Because he didn't fall, the rose didn't grow quite as big or as red as it should have done. Because the rose wasn't quite as big or red, the wedding bouquet it went into didn't look quite as pretty.

Carry this story as far along as seems reasonable to you. Then ask, *Was* it important for the little drop to fall? Is it always important to do our best? If we don't, does it make a difference to others? Give some examples:

(a) A sixth-grader who doesn't do his best. (He may not get into college, may not have as good a job, may not be able to take good care of his family.)

(b) An airplane pilot who doesn't do his best.

(c) A ball-player who doesn't do his best.

(d) A baby-sitter who doesn't do her best.

(e) A ballet student who doesn't do her best.

In each case, talk about how failure to do one's best affects other people negatively, and how they are affected positively when we *do* do our best. Work the conversation around to the concept that people who have many gifts have a great responsibility to use them wisely. Take your time on this part. If you can get this one principle across, the children will feel responsibility for reaching their potential.

5. "*Good, the enemy of best.*" (To help children see that their responsibility is not merely to "get by" but to reach their own personal best.)

Put a sign up somewhere in the house that says, "Good, the enemy of best." Don't say anything about it, but make it prominent enough that the children can't help seeing it and asking about it. Put them off just long enough to heighten their interest; then gather them together and talk about how those who are satisfied just to do a good job never reach—or even discover—their best. Let the children help you think of examples.

6. *Exposure to excellence.* (To help children awaken their latent interests, gifts, talents, and potentials.)

Expose your children to excellence in music, ballet, professional basketball, astronomy, gymnastics—wherever you can find major talent and expertise. If not directly, do so through magazines, books, selected television. Broaden their horizons while you direct them toward excellence. Show them enough variety that they realize the value of finding and being their true selves.

7. *Setting records.* (To help children feel the joy of improving their previous best and to take the responsibility of continuing to do so.)

Make a chart in which you set up a matrix of simple athletic events opposite the children's names, and let each child establish his own personal "record" for each event. Record their best tries and schedule a time for another try. Tell them what they can do to practice in the meantime. Emphasize only the competition with themselves—never competition with one another.

8. *Coping with shyness.* (To help naturally shy children overcome this potential barrier to their potential.)

Some children fail to realize their potential (or even to glimpse it) because of their tendency to be shy and withdrawn and a related tendency not to try or experiment.

Whole books have been written on this subject, of course, but perhaps the simplest and most reliable way to help grade-school children overcome peer shyness is to arrange to have children from their class visit your child to play at your home, followed by a return visit of your child to their home. For a shy child, there is nothing like having a friend over—to play with his toys, to meet his mom, to eat off his plates. The commonality and familiarity make it easier to talk to each other at school.

The best way is to have your child do the inviting. If he is too shy, engineer an exchange visit yourself (parent-to-parent). The results may not be dramatic or immediate, but the shyness will begin to fade.

9. *Family specialists.* (To recognize and reinforce children's individual talents and to provide a way for them to share and experience the higher dimension of learning that comes only in teaching.)

According to aptitude, designate each child to become the "family specialist" in a particular area (such as one for gymnastics, one for violin, one for ballet, one for computers, and so on). Arrange for professional lessons for each child in his specialty, provided that he agrees to come home from those lessons and teach other interested family members what he has learned.

Note: One of the most valuable ways for both parent and child to fulfill their potential (and possibly to cut down on transportation to and from all kinds of lessons) is for parents to teach their own children. Obviously, few parents are qualified to teach a ten-year-old to play the cello. But each parent has a vast store of knowledge to be rediscovered and passed on to the children. When we run out of knowledge or know-how, we can always resort to books written by experts.

C. Family Focal Points: "Weekly Sessions," Family "Major" and "Minor"

In Richard's management consulting career, he has found that the most important tool a businessman can possess is the ability to set and meet appropriate and carefully set goals. His company uses, on its planning sheets and on those it prepares for clients, a simple procedure of filling in a round circle drawn next to each goal to signify its accomplishment or completion.

Recently, as we developed and operated a chain of preschools, we found that the same system, on a more basic level, worked well for three- and four-year-olds. They became as excited about coloring in their circles as the businessmen did. People need progress. We thrive on positive change.

Since our oldest children were three and four years old, we have held "weekly sessions." These are nothing more than a quiet time when each family member thinks about the week ahead, sets some goals, and records those goals on his calendar or plan for the week. Little children simply draw a picture of two goals, putting a circle by each and drawing lines to the days of the week they intend to work on that goal. A slightly older child's completed "weekly session" chart may look like this.

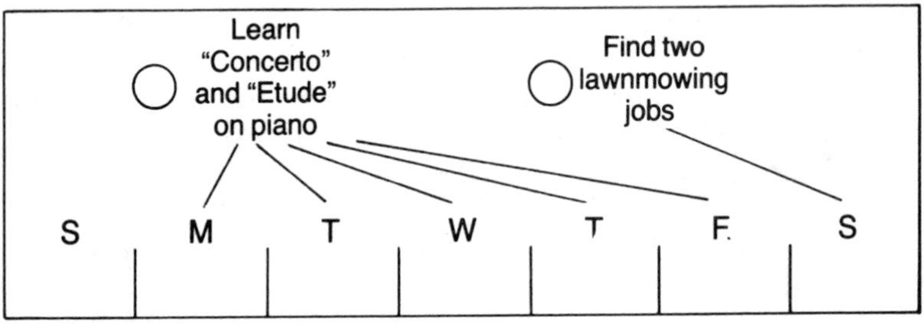

It is important that they understand the difference between a *goal* and a *plan*. For instance, "practicing the piano every day" is not a goal but a plan. The goal may be to learn two new pieces.

In recent years, we have never had to suggest or prompt these weekly sessions. The children prompt us. They want to have them; they want the short talk with their parents where they explain their goals; they want to see their goal diagrams up on the bulletin board; they want to keep track of the days of the week and remember which goal they are working on each day; they want to fill in those circles; they want to bring the completed circles to us at the end of the week.

Once children become interested in setting weekly goals, it is easy to find opportunities to counsel them on what their goals might be. Often the other forms of responsibility we hope to help them accept can find their way into one of their goals. Thus, goal setting is not only a method for teaching the responsibility for potential, but a vehicle for teaching self-commitment on other forms of responsibility as well.

In connection with our weekly sessions, we have the children write in their personal journals. Thus they are looking back over the week just passed as well as forward to the week ahead. One helps with the other, and both help with the children's acceptance of responsibility for potential.

As a framework for our objectives, we have a family "major" and "minor" each year, two things that we are concentrating on together during the year as far as our interests and learning are concerned. One year our major was music and our minor was tennis. We brought home library books on great composers; we related everything we could to these areas of emphasis. Another year the major was painting and graphic art and the minor was the Spanish language.

Deciding on specific areas of focus opens whole new worlds to our children, and it gives them some specific areas of concentration for their weekly goals. Over the years our older children have become remarkably adept at setting and reaching goals. They understand that they can, with perseverance, accomplish any carefully set goal.

To symbolize this, we brought home some silver rings. We gave each of them a ring and showed them that the rings had no end—the circle goes on forever. The rings remind them that there is no end to what they can do. Over time the "family rings" have become a symbol of high goals and noble aspirations.

Feeling the responsibility for potential comes gradually for children, but it can and does come. Some of the methods in this chapter can start the ball rolling, and some of the regular, continuing practices like weekly sessions can keep it rolling.

One final area to consider here is the common concern of parents in helping their children discipline themselves to do the practicing necessary to reach their musical potential. The "war stories" that surround music practice seem to go like this: "I begged my mother to let me quit piano and she did. Now I'd give anything if she hadn't." "My mother forced me to practice for so long and so hard that as soon as I could, I dropped it like a hot potato and haven't touched it since." "I hated not being able to watch television or play with a friend until my practicing was done. My mother used to stand over me with clenched fists, saying, 'Someday you'll thank me for this!' She was right. I'll never be able to thank her enough."

The lingering question is simply: "How do I get my child to practice?" We tried every reward from stars to Saturday movies, but we were still experiencing uprisings and rebellions. I hated dragging children out of their beds and listening to their complaints.

The turning point came when we decided to turn the responsibility over to them. We worked out a plan that was agreeable to all. Everyone knew exactly what was expected in regard to time, place, and length of practice; we offered each a pleasant reward (see chapter 2 on paying children for practice), handed him or her an alarm clock, and said, "Good luck!"

Slowly but surely they became much more consistent in practicing—so much so that we can hardly believe our eyes! As their latent talent began to emerge, we found real joy in talking to them about the wonderful potential they had for music and their responsibility to develop it.

Section 3 Summary Story

Back to the Thompson family. As they completed their first three months on this section of the book (Responsibility to Self), Dan and Corry began to see glimpses of real discipline and self-reliance in their children. They were surprised almost to the point of shock to see their ten-year-old getting up early to practice his music. They were pleased with the new and more serious and analytical way their children viewed decisions and choices. Perhaps most noticeably, they were excited about the children's ability to set some simple goals each week, and about their interest in being responsible for those goals and for reaching them.

Their only concern was that there seemed to be little continuity or conscious connection in the children's minds between their decisions and their goals, or between the goals they set one week and the ones they set the following week. Dan and Corry were anxious that the children see their decisions and goals as ways to reach their potential and as the means to developing a good character. They felt a need to tie these things together in their children's minds and teach them that what they did each week was one small step in a staircase leading to what they could become and to what they could contribute. At the same time, Dan and Corry knew they had to keep things simple. If they made the weekly sessions of setting goals any more complicated, it would ruin them.

What they finally came up with was simple, and it worked:

1. They got each child a special loose-leaf binder and put his or her name on the front. They called the books "My Life

Plan" and put five dividers in them labeled "Lifetime Goals," "One-Year Goals," "One-Month Goals," "Weekly Goals," and "Decisions in Advance."

2. They spent several hours one day helping each of the children get their "Life Plan" books started. They helped them begin their list of lifetime goals in the first section ("have a family," "have a good job," "probably be an architect," "be a good musician," and so forth). They helped them choose some simple yearly goals that pointed toward those lifetime goals (get through Book 6 in Piano Series, get more than half A's each quarter in school). Then they helped them transpose the yearly goals down to dovetailing one-month goals (read a specific book, learn a concerto, make two new friends). Finally, they made sure the children understood the relationships between the various levels of objectives, and realized that the goals they set each week were simply the things they could do to get to the monthly goals.

In the last section, each child started a list of decisions he was willing to make in advance (see chapter 7). Once the books were set up, weekly goal setting became much easier and more fun. The children were able to see how what they did each week contributed to what they could achieve that month, and that monthly goals led to yearly achievements, which brought them closer to their lifetime goals.

Over time, other things were added to the life plan books, including descriptions written by the children of the *type* of person they hoped to be in five years. The children began to bring their books to their weekly interviews with their parents, and to take pride in their own abilities to chart a course for their lives.

Dan and Corry decided to add one more dimension to the Thompsonville Family Bank to tie it in with the children's weekly goals. They explained that each week a child met all his goals, he would get a special bonus when that week's "pay" was counted up for his points.

The typing in of weekly goals with the family bank system and with longer-range goals gave more of the initiative to the children and made a noticeable difference in the amount of responsibility they felt to themselves.

SECTION 4

RESPONSIBILITY TO OTHERS

When responsibility becomes associated with service, it takes on even higher qualities. To feel responsible to parents and authority figures, and later to self, is obedience and maturity, but to feel responsible to others is love—responsibility of the purest form and the highest dimension.

Section 2 dealt with responsibility to mankind, or to other people collectively as part of society. This section deals with responsibility to others as individuals. When we accept responsibility that is not our obligation, when we take on burdens that should belong to others, then we begin to develop true greatness of character.

Even the most mature adult finds it difficult to think consistently in terms of responsibility for others, so how can we possibly teach that concept to children? The truth is that they may well be more adept at learning it than adults are. At least until they become teenagers, they are usually more flexible, less affected by the selfishness and self-centeredness of the world. Thus they can feel responsibility for others. They need only to be pointed in the right direction.

Responsibility for Smaller Children 10

TENNIS
TENNIS

The point at which older children start becoming part of the solution rather than part of the problem is the point at which families move into a higher realm of calmness and order.

The goal of good parents is to turn children into good parents.

A. Definition and Illustration

About the time they turn eight, most children experience strong desires to begin the transition from child to adult. They want to be treated as adults, to have the opportunities of adults; and, while they probably won't admit it, they want some of the *responsibilities* of adults. One of the clearest and most demonstrable ways to separate them from little children is to give them some responsibilities for smaller children in the family.

The old adage "You don't really learn until you teach" has great merit. By molding your older children into teachers for the younger ones, you do three things: (1) lighten *your* load; (2) let the younger ones be taught more than you could teach them on your own; and (3) bring about the ultimate learning experience for the older children, who learn by teaching.

Todd and Sally had always wanted a large family, and their circumstances were comfortable enough to allow it. They lived in a rural area with lots of space. Todd's salary was adequate to support a large family. Sally bore children easily. They had six children in eight years. And their children were bright, precocious, and strong willed.

Just lately, the responsibilities for so many children had really caught up with Todd and Sally. Demands for time and attention often seemed physically impossible. Just sitting at the dinner table and trying to talk all at once to the four who could talk, in between feeding and changing the two little ones, was a harrowing experience. Todd and Sally needed help. Six small children for two adults to handle seemed overwhelming.

One night while they were out to dinner, a new and different idea occurred to Todd and Sally. Though they were trying not to think about the children, the pressure of the six-to-two ratio kept coming up in their conversation.

"You know, if we could just turn one of those kids into an

adult, take one away from their side and add one to our side, it would be five to three—not nearly such bad odds." Todd was doing some mental meandering, just thinking out loud.

Sally kept the thought going. "Well, Judith is eight. She's old enough to take some responsibility. Maybe we ought to recruit her over to our side—tell her that from now on she's on our team and shares the adult responsibilities."

Todd, a stockbroker, became intrigued with the numbers. "Hey, in ten more months, Terry will be eight. If we can recruit him too, we would even up the battle with four to a side!"

What started off as a rambling and only half-serious thought became more important and more feasible as they discussed it.

Later that week, they sat down to discuss the situation with Judith. They made it seem like a graduation. They congratulated Judith for reaching a point of maturity where she could become one of the three "grown-ups" in the family. They told her that she would now be included in lots of new things: she would be included in the special weekly planning meeting that Mom and Dad always held; she would be able to stay up for an extra half hour each night; she would be able to sit with the grown-ups instead of the children at Thanksgiving dinner and other times when relatives came over; and she would be able to start taking care of the other children more, just as Mom and Dad did.

Judith was thrilled and proud. She took on a slightly different demeanor from that moment; she seemed to stand a little taller, to look a little older.

The next morning at breakfast when things got a little wild, Sally asked Judith to change the baby instead of trying to do it herself. When Billy needed help finding his shoes, Judith did it. When everyone talked at once, Sally told some of them to ask their questions of Judith instead of her. That evening Todd and Sally, with Judith's help, put the other children to bed and left Judith to baby-sit while they went out for a while. Actually, they didn't go far, and they came back at least once to peek in the window and see how things were going, but they *did* go out, and they *did* leave Judith in charge.

With meaningful looks and warm words, they praised Judith for her new role. They thanked her and let her know honestly and sincerely that she was making their lives happier.

They also prodded the children to say thank you to their big sister more often.

It worked. The ratio was five to three. And a few months later it was four to four. But nine *more* months later it was five to four—the children were ahead again.

B. Methods

1. *Helping younger siblings to change clothes.* (To help small children feel the satisfaction of helping the still smaller ones.)

One of the earliest opportunities for children to help their younger brothers and sisters comes in the clothes-changing area. A four-year-old who can dress himself can also help a two-year-old get dressed. With a lavish amount of praise as their reward, it is amazing how much children enjoy offering and giving this help.

Making it into a race can keep this activity interesting. One evening you might say to your four-year-old son, Jason, "Let's time you and see how fast you can get your pajamas on and be back out here in the living room. You'll need to put your clothes away in the drawer, too. Ready, set, go!"

After the fun of setting and breaking records is established, say, "Okay, Jason, tonight I think you're old enough to try a new kind of record. Let's see how long it takes both you and Jimmy to get your pajamas on. Okay, Jimmy? Jason, you'll have to help Jimmy a lot. Can you do it?"

The praise has to be increased for this double accomplishment. Jason needs to feel not only the satisfaction of getting something done fast, but also of being big enough to help his little brother do it. Say such things as, "You know, Jason, I think you got Jimmy ready faster than *I* could have."

Remember to praise Jimmy, too, so that he will continue to be cooperative in the joint venture.

2. *The "buddy system."* (To help children feel responsibility at certain times for their younger brothers and sisters, and to keep from losing one of them when you are in a public place.)

In a large family, let the children pair off with each other as buddies so that they stay in twos and don't get split off or lost in public places. In a smaller family, an older child can be assigned to a younger one. In either case, the key is to emphasize the responsibility of the older child in the pair and to give generous praise after the fact for the good job he has done.

3. *Teaching opportunities.* (To develop children's teaching skills and to allow them to feel their ability to mold and influence their younger brothers and sisters.)

Try saying something like this: "Jared, I've been noticing how much Timmy follows your example. He does everything you do. He really looks up to you. I guess a nine-year-old is pretty big to a four-year-old. I think you can really help me with something. You see, Timmy just cannot seem to learn to keep his closet straight. His shoes are always left out or just thrown in. If he were in the same room as you, he'd see how neat you are and then do the same. Since he isn't, he doesn't have a good example. I've tried to teach him, but I think you could do it better than I. Would you teach Timmy how to arrange his closet so it's neat and tidy, and would you teach him to keep it that way? Thanks, son, I really appreciate it. It's surely nice to have a boy as big and as helpful as you!"

4. *Paid baby-sitting.* (To help children feel and accept the same kind of responsibility that they have seen their baby-sitters accepting.)

Most children have observed, over the years, the responsible position of their baby-sitters. Baby-sitters receive instructions from parents and have authority; they are important. Telling a nine- or ten-year-old that he is old enough to baby-sit can generate real excitement. Phrase it in a totally positive and complimentary way: "Baby-sitting is usually only for older children, and it does pay money. Since we have a very responsible child in our family who is growing up so fast, we thought we might let you start baby-sitting a little earlier than most."

Give clear, simple instructions. Leave a telephone number where you can be reached. If you will not be close by, leave the number of a neighbor with whom you have made previous arrangements.

Pay the child a small hourly wage as soon as you get home, and accompany it with a great deal of praise.

An occasional baby-sitting experience in which a child feels complete responsibility for his younger brothers and sisters will greatly increase the responsibility he feels for them from day to day.

5. *"Simon Says" game and discussion.* (To impress upon older children how much of what they do influences the behavior of their little brothers and sisters.)

Play "Simon Says" with the children. Let the older children be Simon most of the time.

When the game is over, take the older ones aside and discuss what the little children did when no one said "Simon says." Bring up examples of the smaller children following them, in good things as well as bad. Use the word *responsibility* often in your discussion.

6. *Your interaction with older children.* (To dramatize the differences in your family between the younger children and the older "responsibility takers.")

Many parents adopt a particular way of talking to children. It is usually a loving way, involving slower speech and smaller words, perhaps a little patronizing, and sometimes using baby talk. Often we stay with that style of communicating when our children are too old for it.

When speaking with your children who are old enough to have been given some responsibility for the others, make a conscious, obvious change. Speak to them as you would an adult. Talk at a normal rate, in a normal tone, with normal expression. The difference is often quite noticeable. Children will respond. As in everything, they will live up to your expectation and recognition of their maturity, communicated not so much by what you say but by how you say it.

7. "*Parenthood training.*" (To strengthen children's desire to accept more responsibility for siblings.)

Since you are their parent, one of the most complimentary things you can say to your children is that you think they will someday be good parents.

If they balk at the responsibilities you are giving them for their brothers and sisters, remind them that they too will someday be mothers and fathers, and that the things they do for the other children help not only the little children, but help *them* also in getting ready to be good parents themselves.

Obviously, parents can carry this too far and put too much responsibility on children. Sometimes the oldest child in a family is given too much responsibility, the others too little.

8. "*Tutors.*" (To cause children to feel responsibility for a younger child for an extended period.)

At the beginning of the month, take an older child aside and say something like this: "Jerry, there are two or three things that Stevie really needs help on. Since he looks up to you so much, we thought you might be the one to help him. He needs to learn to keep his room cleaner, and he needs to mind Mom better. We would like to give you a challenge. It's the first of November today. By Thanksgiving, let's see if you can help him to be better on both things."

Talk about how Jerry can do it. Discuss the importance of example, as well as how he might remind Stevie. Discuss how he might bring Stevie into his own room and proudly show him how clean it is. Give Jerry a lot of helpful ideas and then praise him and remind him often as the month passes.

Once children begin to learn to discipline themselves, a wonderful thing happens: they become capable of being responsible for others. This is a necessary and joyous transition for many families.

We discovered the joys of this transition when our oldest daughter was about six. She had been taught using the methods in *Teaching Children Joy* as we wrote the book and tried its ideas on her. One day we found her out in the woods beside our house teaching her little brother and sister about the joy of the earth. She didn't know we were listening. In her own sweet way she told them all about the beautiful autumn leaves. She pointed out the joy of the squirrels in the tree, the design in the tree bark, and the sound of the birds, all in a very meaningful and clear manner.

You never really know how much of what you teach your children is being internalized until you hear it come out again. We felt exhilarated—as though we were watching a baby's first step, only better.

Opportunities should be sought every day to find ways for children to teach. Encourage them to prepare special family presentations on a topic of their choice, complete with visual aids. You'll be amazed at their creativity and effectiveness.

C. Family Focal Point: The Age-Eight Transition

When our children turn eight, they undergo the "passage" aspects that we have referred to earlier, and three rather clear and regular manifestations of their new position begin almost immediately:

1. *Paid baby-sitting.* In our case, they have been waiting for this opportunity and know that it is not only a chance to earn

money, but a sign that they have become part of the adult side of our family.

2. *Teaching time.* Once a week we try to get all of the family together for stories or a brief lesson on something we feel is important. We have a particular way of handling this time that we think helps our older children accept responsibility for the younger ones. We call it "pass-it-along-teaching."

We take our older children (those over the age of eight) and have a separate meeting with them while the smaller children play. We teach the idea or tell the story we have prepared in an adult way. Then we assign each of the older ones to teach the lesson to the younger ones. We then convene as a family, with parents serving only to keep things organized and the little ones attentive while the older children teach.

3. *Executive session portion of "weekly sessions."* As discussed earlier, we devote some time each week to planning the coming week. One segment of this time, held in the evening, is the adult part. Originally it was just for the parents, coordinating our own weekly schedules and discussing our objectives for the week ahead. As some of the children got older, we began to include them and to devote some of the time to talking about the smaller children, what their special needs were, and how we could help them. It still surprises us how much insight our older children have about their little brothers and sisters.

We also sometimes take the older children along for a "four-facet review" of the smaller ones (see chapter 5).

Responsibility for Dependability 11

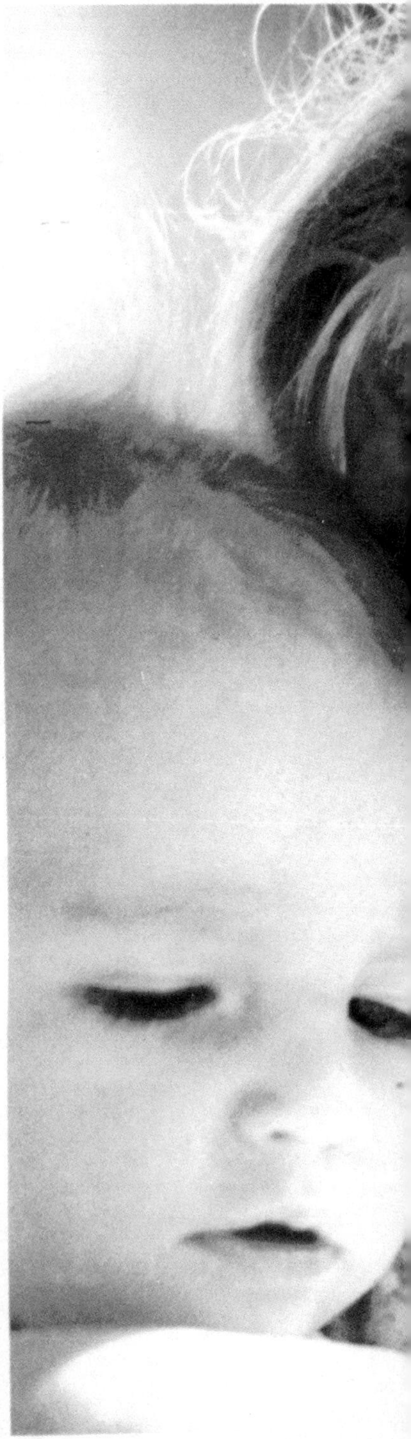

Responsibility for Dependability 11

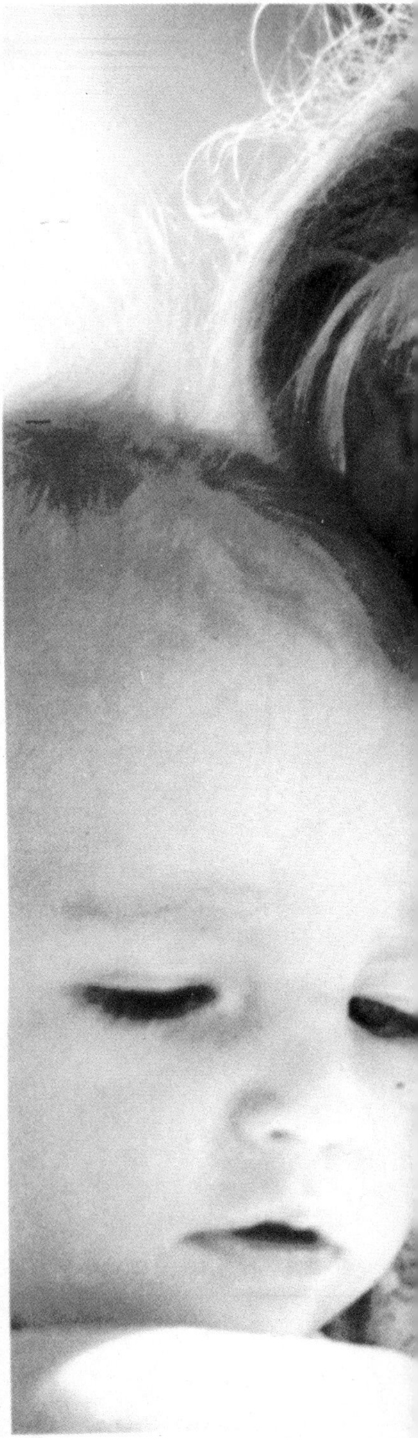

In an adult, dependability is the fruit of true maturity; in a child, it is the seed.

A. *Definition and Illustration*

There are many shades of meaning for the word *dependability*. It is a quality all of us admire, all of us want in ourselves and in our associates. On its most basic level, it means honesty—doing what you say you will do. On its higher level, it also means saying you will do the *right* things—making commitments and keeping them even when it is not easy and when it requires personal sacrifice.

By the time Martha Curtis turned eleven, she was an absolute model of dependability. Her mother, Larie, said she would rather leave the baby with Martha than with her husband. Martha followed instructions. She looked around and saw what needed to be done. She kept her mind on what she was doing. She had been that way as long as Larie could remember.

Martha had a twin sister named Marian. Marian was unidentical in every way. Larie called her "the artist" because it was the most complimentary way she could think of to describe Marian's erratic, spontaneous, totally unpredictable and undependable personality.

When Larie and her husband, Ben, went out, they told Martha to be responsible for Marian, and she was.

As the girls grew older, Marian's unpredictable behavior became less and less amusing and more and more worrisome. She never seemed to get something done when she was asked. She constantly showed up at school without her assignments; she wasn't obstinate or rebellious—she simply forgot. She couldn't keep things in her mind, and she couldn't keep her mind on things. The better Martha got, the worse Marian became.

One weekend Ben and Larie had a surprise visit from Bill and Treena, old school friends. They went out for dinner, and the discussion turned to children. Treena, who hadn't seen the twins for eight years, said, "Are those two girls still the same—Marian a free spirit with her mind going in a hundred different directions, and Martha a model of perfect behavior and orderliness?"

"Is that your description or mine?" Larie asked.

"Well, both, I guess," said Treena, somewhat puzzled. "That's just how I remember them, but come to think of it, that *is* exactly how you used to describe the two of them."

When they got home that night, Larie and Ben started thinking. Apparently they had been reinforcing a particular personality type in each girl since before the twins were three years old. As they talked, they realized that they had never really given Marian much chance to be dependable. They had paid so much attention to her spontaneity and flightiness that she had simply bent further and further in that direction.

There was only one thing to do—start over. Clearly, what they didn't want to do was to take away any of Marian's spontaneity; it wasn't really a question of removing anything, just *adding* something.

Larie and Ben went to work on it. They started with very basic forms of dependability, using several methods in this chapter. They moved slowly, not expecting dependability in more than one area at a time. And gradually, Marian began to catch on. She began to see the cause and effect between commitments and results, between priorities and efficiency, between how dependable she was and how much people trusted her.

Larie watched, encouraged, and praised her at every opportunity. At the same time, she gave extra attention to Martha too, used her as an example and helper in teaching Marian certain things, consciously avoiding making her feel resentful or left out. Ben and Larie began to realize that certain methods and techniques were helpful in getting Marian to understand and desire dependability, but that praise, reputation, and positive attention were what really brought about and sustained actual changes.

B. Methods

1. *Integration of the dependability-emphasis into methods previously discussed in other chapters.*

(a) *Ancestor stories.* Look for incidents from your life or your parents' or grandparents' lives that demonstrate reliability. Compose those incidents into children's stories, emphasizing that those qualities of reliability and dependability are genetically and environmentally passed on to you and to your children.

(b) "*Weekly sessions.*" Setting weekly goals, as children do in the weekly sessions, is a dependability-building activity. As children follow through and accomplish what they committed themselves to the week before, they are developing a sense of reliability to themselves and to others.

By making dependability a topic in the weekly sessions, you can teach the concept even further. As the children plan their weeks, ask them if they have any assignments, if they have made any arrangements or commitments with or to anyone else. Put any such commitments on their calendars and use them as an opportunity to talk about how important it is to be reliable, to do whatever we have agreed to do.

(c) *Four-facet review.* As you review monthly each child's social progress, focus your attention (especially during the month you are concentrating on this chapter) on how dependable each child is. Think back over each child's development and try to identify any trends toward or away from dependability. As always, just thinking about it and focusing on it will bring to your minds some ideas for improvement.

(d) *Reinforcement.* As with every form of responsibility, the most effective and useful method of all is to watch for any instance where a child exhibits reliability or dependability and to praise him lavishly.

2. *The Dependable or Undependable game.* (To help children learn to see the effects of dependability, or the lack of it, on others.)

Make up two signs, each on a sheet of cardboard with a string that can go around your neck so that you can wear the sign. Have one sign say *Dependable* and the other *Undependable.* If both parents are there, each should wear one. If not, an older child may wear one.

Then have the children play the role of someone who is depending on you—a teacher, a friend, a neighbor. You respond to them according to your sign. For example:

A teacher (role-played by one of the children) asks you to give an extra-credit report on a book the class has been studying. *Dependable* prepares and gives an interesting report. *Undependable* forgets. In the first case the teacher is pleased and gives the student a good grade. In the second case the teacher is unhappy, the class does not run smoothly, and *Undependable* misses a chance for extra points.

A friend lends you his baseball glove. You tell him you will bring it to the game on Friday. *Dependable* remembers; *Undependable* not only forgets the glove—he forgets the game.

A neighbor family is going to be away for the summer and agrees to pay you to cut, water, and care for their lawn while they are away. *Dependable* does it as regularly and as well as if the family were there watching. *Undependable* waits until the lawn is dry before he waters it and until it's up to his ankles before he cuts it.

Add more examples according to your own imagination and your own children's needs. Focus the game on how the one who has given you the responsibility feels when he is let down and how he feels when the responsibility is dependably kept.

3. *Making reliability a family tradition.* (To commit yourselves, as a family and as individuals within a family, to be absolutely reliable and dependable.)

The Dependable or Undependable game and any ancestor stories you may have found illustrating dependability will set the stage for a family commitment to reliability. Discuss the ramifications of being reliable and how it affects others and yourselves. Propose that reliability become a family tradition. Talk about situations in the children's lives where it will apply immediately: school assignments, music practice, and so forth.

Write the word *reliability* on a sign of some kind and put it up in the kitchen or dining room where you eat your evening meal. During the month you spend on this chapter, discuss at dinner anything that has happened that day to any family member that illustrates dependability or that provided an opportunity to demonstrate dependability.

4. *The priorities game.* (To help children think about the relative, long-range importance of certain things and differentiate between things of true importance and those of only momentary significance.)

Prepare in advance on simple three-by-five-inch cards a list, one to a card, of things that differ vastly in terms of their ultimate importance. Examples:

(a) A new dress.
(b) How easy or how difficult it is to talk to your parents about important matters.

(c) Being elected to the student council.
(d) Watching your favorite television show.
(e) Your grades in school.
(f) Learning to love good literature.
(g) How kind you are to your brothers and sisters.
(h) How hard you practice your piano lessons.
(i) How many friends you have.
(j) How well you treat your friends.

Pick the items that are timely and relevant to your family's current situation. Color code the *back* of each card with either a yellow, a red, or a blue dot. Put yellow on the back of items that are so important that they can affect our character (items b, f, g, and j above). Put a red dot on those items that might affect how happy we will be ten years from now (items e, h, and i). Put a blue dot on those that are either not important at all or that matter for only a short while (items a, c, and d).

Depending on which items you choose and the level of understanding of your children, some might have a dot of one color plus the trace of a second color. For instance, "your grades in school" might have a red dot but also a trace of yellow because reaching our full potential affects our character.

Put the cards, colored dot facing down, on the table and see if the children can arrange them in descending order to the least important. Then turn the cards all over and see if all the yellows are together at the top, followed by the reds, and then the blues. The stage will be set for a good discussion.

5. *Making others your priority.* (To help children connect the concept of dependability to others.)

Children need to understand that dependability is a responsibility to others, that their motivation for becoming dependable should be not merely to improve their own characters and personalities, but to actually help others, to make others more comfortable and more secure.

Go back to the priorities game (method 4) and add some cards to the stack, such as, finishing school assignments, helping someone in need, keeping promises, and volunteering for service in the community. Each time dependability and reliability to other people are involved, the card should get a yellow mark and be arranged in the game as a high priority.

6. *Review their "advance decision list."* (To use the commitments that children have made to themselves and to you as illustrations of the two parts of dependability: making good

commitments and keeping them. See the "family focal points" section of chapter 7.)

Praise the children for the correctness of the decisions they have made and tell them how appropriate it is that they have committed themselves to their decisions by writing them down and signing them. Help them see that what they have done by making the list is the first step in dependability. Explain that keeping those commitments is the second step. Discuss how they are doing on each one and whether they still think the decisions are correct ones. Talk about the strength of each commitment and if the children feel they will be dependable in keeping it.

7. *Your own commitment list.* (To give children the reassurance and example of seeing your own personal commitments.)

In the "family focal points" section are some illustrations of the types of commitments that couples may wish to make to each other and with each other. If you write these commitments down and read them to your children, it will bolster and strengthen their desire both to make and to keep commitments of their own.

8. *Your own marriage and family commitment.* (To help children understand what unconditional commitment is and to give them the security of knowing that you are always totally committed to each other and to them.)

Tell your children the story of your courtship and marriage. Discuss the fact that marriage is a commitment to be partners all your life. Tell them how much you depend on each other and how hard you try to be dependable to each other. Point out that the more things they can be dependable in now, the more prepared they will be to be dependable in their own commitment of marriage later on.

C. Family Focal Point: Commitment Lists

People who are absolutely dependable, who do what they say they will (and more), who see what needs doing and do it without specific directives, are rare. Richard once had a business partner who fit the mold. He never worried about something when his partner had charge of it. He knew that whatever could be done would be done, and felt relaxed and reassured. He now has a secretary-assistant, someone who manages a particular operation who is totally dependable. She needs no follow-up or reminders. Whatever he thinks of, she has thought of it first, and done it. When he gives her something to do, or they decide together to take some particular step, he can consider it done as of that moment.

It is wonderful to work with people like this. The only thing more wonderful is to have that kind of dependability within a marriage and family, to have an inner confidence in each other that never fades, even in moments of stress or disagreement.

We are convinced that this kind of reliability comes to a family as the parents and children make certain commitments to themselves and other commitments between each other.

People essentially want to commit themselves to something. They want the direction, security, and peace of mind that commitment brings. As the concept of commitment became more and more appealing to us, we decided to formalize some of the commitments we had made over the years. The list that emerged looked, in part, like this:

Commitment to *oneness* (sharing everything with each other)

Commitment to *simplicity* (avoiding things unrelated to joy)

Commitment to *seeking* (actively looking for our highest potential)

Commitment to *service* (looking for it and giving it)

Commitment to *priorities* (to base every decision on them)

Commitment to *planning* (to live life on yearly, monthly, and weekly goals)

The list represents commitments to each other, to others in and outside of our family, to certain values, to particular ways of behaving, to individual preferences. It has become a part of our identity and our life pattern.

As our children become old enough, we invite them to join us in certain of our collective commitments and to make others of their own and share them with us. The prerequisite, of course, is a thorough understanding of the meaning of the word *commitment.* For our family's purposes, it is defined as something one has thought about carefully and decided as a free individual to do. A certain unspoken honor system is involved. Children know they should not *sign* a commitment (we do sign them) unless they really intend to keep it in all circumstances.

Much of the dependability we hope to build in our children stems from the commitments they have made. In some cases their commitments relate directly to dependable behavior, such as a commitment to be truthful and a commitment to complete whatever task they are given. But all commitments build dependability as they are kept, because the essence of dependability is compatibility between what one says he will do and what he does.

In addition, family commitment lists are a great teaching method for other forms of responsibility: commitment to obedience, to order, to honorable actions, and so forth.

Responsibility for Contributing 12

The most beautiful of all forms of give-and-take is when one takes *the responsibility to* give.

A. Definition and Illustration

Some things—and they happen to be the world's most valuable things—work in opposition to the natural law of depletion. We have more of these to give as we give more away: love, perspective, inner beauty.

The irony of these special things is that their proper use and management erases the usual distinctions between selfishness and selflessness. If someone wants more love (a selfish phrase) he can obtain it by giving more love (a selfless phrase). If he wants to give stronger courage to someone else (selfless), he has to develop stronger courage for himself (selfish).

The beauty of the subject matter of this concluding chapter is that it fits this same pattern. If we want our children to receive, obtain, and have much care from others, much concern, much courage, much attention, much recognition—in short, much love—we must help them to take responsibility for contributing those same things *to* the lives of others.

The goal of this chapter is to help you help your children feel responsible not only for what they have, but for contributing it to the world that surrounds them.

Sean was the kind of child who attracts attention and love like a magnet. From the day he was born he was a strikingly beautiful child with thick, blond curls, pale blue eyes, and the face of a cherub. Life seemed easy for Sean. He walked early, talked early, and made friends so easily that, at three years of age, he seemed always to be surrounded by other children, always the center of attention.

When he started school it was the same. His teachers loved him, and other children followed him around and courted his friendship. He excelled in his studies, and in extracurricular activities, from art to sports, he was always a leader. Yet his was a natural, easy kind of superiority that endeared him to others rather than offending or arousing jealousy.

About the time he turned nine, Sean came to a major decision. He didn't realize it, but he stood at a fork in the road. One option was to take it easy and let life, which always seemed to work in his favor, take its course. He had shown some leanings toward that direction lately. He was slightly bored with life and with how easy it was, and there were some things, like homework, that he just didn't bother to do. Life wasn't very challenging. The other option was to start thinking in terms of leadership, to start challenging himself not in a competitive sense, but in a contributing sense.

While Sean was not consciously aware of the two alternatives he was facing, his parents were. They had watched their son closely. They knew that the usual challenges of life were not enough for him, and they knew it was essential that he think of himself as one who carried the responsibility of example, of leadership, and of contributing to the world around him.

Rather than trying to explain all this to Sean in theoretical terms, they decided on a more specific, pragmatic approach. One evening they initiated a particularly important conversation that went something like this:

Dad: "Sean, is there anyone in your class at school who is a real outcast—someone no one talks to or no one plays with?"

Sean: "No. Oh, yes, there is Perry. He's new this year, and he just doesn't fit in. He talks kind of funny, he wears weird clothes, and he keeps to himself."

Mom: "Does he keep to himself, Sean, or do other kids just avoid him so he has to be by himself? Think about that for a minute before you answer."

Sean: "Yeah, I think you're right. People do avoid him."

Dad: "Sean, in a way we were kind of hoping you had someone like that in your class. We want to give you a challenge—a challenge to be a real friend to Perry. You know you are a boy that everyone likes. Everyone wants to be your friend. With Perry it is just the opposite—imagine how that would feel."

Mom: "Son, we've talked about this before, but you know you are especially talented. You're good at many things. You have a chance to use those gifts to help other people and to make their lives happier."

Dad: "So that's our challenge to you, Sean, to make Perry happy, to be his good friend. Can you do it?"

Sean: (A long pause, then a smile.) "Sure I can do it."

Mom: "What were you thinking about just then, son?"

Sean: "I was just thinking that if I start being really nice to Perry, I bet the other kids will too."

Dad: "That's just what we've been thinking, Sean. That's quite a responsibility you have."

Sean: "I guess so. You know, though, Dad, Perry is a hard guy to like. He's kind of sloppy, and he acts like he doesn't like anyone."

Mom: "Maybe the way he acts is *proof* of how much love and friendship he needs."

Sean: "I think I understand."

Sean's prediction was right. As he started being friendly to Perry, other children did too. It took a few days. At first, when Sean picked Perry when they were choosing up for kickball, he got some strange looks and a couple of snickers. And when he sat by Perry on the bus and put his arm around his shoulder while they were walking to the lunchroom, there were a few comments and wisecracks. By the end of the week, though, boys and girls who wanted to be around Sean found themselves also around Perry, and Perry turned out to be not such a bad fellow after all.

Most importantly, the incident set a pattern in Sean's life. With a lot of help from his parents, he began to find that he was happiest when he was contributing or helping. Partly because he liked long words, *contributing* became his favorite. By the time he was ten and a half, Sean was consciously and fairly consistently looking for ways to help people, to fill needs, to give service.

We have always asked our children to care for the unfortunate and to watch out for those in need. During Shawni's third-grade year, she became acutely aware of a little girl in her class who was being mistreated and was always misbehaving. Shawni came home almost every night with a horror story about Belinda. "Today she had to stay in the classroom while the rest of us went to the assembly." "Today she threw up in the lunchroom." "Today she didn't get any treats because she is allergic to candy." "No one will play with Belinda."

We suggested that she make Belinda her friend, and we'd see if we could help her. Belinda responded to a birthday invitation. By the time she arrived at the party, our whole family could hardly wait to meet the famous (or should we say infamous) Belinda.

She arrived at the door a little early, obviously excited to be there. After hearing her first few remarks, we could see that she was nine going on seventeen and extremely hyperactive. She covered every inch of our house within fifteen minutes and had asked every family member at least twelve questions as though she were the inspector in an Agatha Christie play. During the party games she spent most of her time on her own, playing with toys she "found" in the back room, breaking an arm off one of our daughter's beloved dolls, and taking five dollars out of Shawni's "treasure chest." Yet when it was present-opening and refreshment time, she was right at Shawni's side, beaming in the glory of her newfound friendship.

The next day I called one of her teachers and was told, as I had suspected, that she did have some physical problems and was being abused at home. So we persevered. The next time Shawni asked her over to play, Belinda broke several toys and disappeared on one of the children's bikes for half an hour. Shawni and I sat down with her and explained to her our family laws, our real concern for her as a friend, and her need to follow our laws while she was at our house.

She did not become perfect, but she improved. She also sent innumerable notes to Shawni telling her how much she liked her and everything about her. She listed everything from "You are good at handwriting" to "You are my friend."

Shawni learned a great deal from that experience. She learned that when children have problems at school, it usually stems from problems at home or may be attributed to health problems. She learned that the choice of friends should involve not only people who can help *us,* but people whom we can help. As she saw other children in the class begin to accept Belinda, Shawni also learned some basic principles of leadership.

B. Methods

1. *Methods to help small children understand the concept of service and feel the actual satisfaction of helping another person.*

(a) *Story: "The Sharing Tree."* (This story, from *Teaching Children Joy,* defines some terms and prepares children for other methods.)

"Please don't make me push them any further," little Oakley pleaded. "It's so cold and damp down there, and I keep bumping into rocks." The baby oak tree was about to cry when

Oakhurst, the grand old oak standing beside him, explained again, "Now, Oakley, my son, soon it will be spring, with hard spring winds, and then summer, with summer storms. Your roots must be strong to hold the rest of you in place. They must be deep in the rich, moist soil to find nourishing food to make your trunk and branches sturdy and healthy. By next year you will have grown so much, you won't believe it!" "Very well," sighed Oakley with a sad but determined grunt. He pushed his roots deeper into the ground, a little further each day, until spring arrived.

One warm, beautiful spring day, Oakley glanced over at his branches and was amazed to see beautiful green buds all over his tips. He thought they were gorgeous, and he was feeling great until one day he started to feel that his beautiful buds were about to burst. "Oh, Oakhurst," he gasped as he looked at his magnificent friend beside him, "my branches, my beautiful branches! They're about to burst and I can't stop them, no matter how hard I try!" "My dear Oakley," smiled the big, calm tree, "stop trying! Instead of losing something, you'll find a pleasant surprise. You must learn that when you let go of something precious to you, it will be replaced by something better." Because he trusted his kind friend so much, Oakley reluctantly let go. Almost like hundreds of little jack-in-the-boxes, tiny green leaves began to appear all over his branches. "Oh, look at me now!" Oakley cried. "You were right!"

As days passed, Oakley became more and more beautiful. He loved the feeling of the wind rustling through his leaves, but the thing that made him happiest was to watch the family of robins who had built their home in his branches. They were happy there, and that made Oakley happy too. He was so glad that he was strong and sturdy with deep roots and that he was sharing with others the beauty and comfort of his leaves. Before long he noticed little brown seeds beginning to form, which Oakhurst told him were acorns; he was proud of them, too.

One day as he was watching the robin children play, he noticed that his leaves were not so green. Some had even begun to turn gold, and one of his acorns fell off, and then another, and then another and another. "Stop!" he screamed. "I need you all to keep me beautiful!" But they continued to fall, and he shouted, "Oakhurst, what is happening? I'm changing color, and my acorns are falling!" "Don't be afraid," said Oakhurst kindly. "Remember what I said to you before. Any time you give up something special to you, you are giving service, and it will always be replaced by something better. Soon you will lose all your acorns. Many of them will be gathered up by our little friends the squirrels, who will store them for food for the winter so they won't be hungry when all the berries have gone. Some will even find a warm spot in the earth, and then when spring comes, they will sprout roots of their own and begin to grow. And you'll find that you'll turn from green to gorgeous orange and red, and then the weather will turn cold and you'll lose all your leaves." "Lose all my leaves!" shrieked Oakley. "Then I will be ugly and cold and I'll never grow to be so wise and beautiful as *you*." "Ah, you are wrong, my little friend," said the grand old Oakhurst. "That's exactly how I became wise and strong."

At the time, Oakley thought that was all very strange, but as the days passed he began to realize what his friend meant. He saw his acorns drop and his little friends gather them for winter food. His leaves turned a beautiful red, and then, just as Oakhurst had said, they began to drop off. He was sad at first, but when he saw the children rustling through them and having so much fun playing in them, he was glad for the opportunity to share. And when the cold winter came (and Oakley did look a bit ugly some days), he was happy that he had shared himself. He knew that when springtime came again he would be stronger, his roots would be longer, his leaves and branches would be bigger, and he would be better and more like his great friend Oakhurst.

(b) *Story: "Alice Learns about Sharing."*

In mid-December, a new little girl came into Alice's class. She was smaller than Alice and rather thin, but pretty with large, brown eyes and dark hair. Her dress was too big for her, and though it was clean, it looked old and worn. Her name was Heather. She sat right next to Alice. The two little girls quickly became friends, and after school, Heather asked Alice if she could come to her house to play. They stopped at Alice's house to ask her mother, and then went on to Heather's house.

Alice noticed as they walked along that Heather didn't have any boots or gloves and that her coat was thin. She held her coat tightly around her because the zipper was broken.

Heather lived in a small gray house with her grandmother, who was quite old and who looked tired and worried.

Alice said, "Let's play house. What kind of dolls do you have?"

Heather said, "I have only this one doll, but you can use it and you can be the mommy." It was a small rag doll with only one arm and no clothes. Heather said, "I asked my grandmother if I could have a new doll for my birthday, but she said she didn't even have enough money for food, and she couldn't buy a doll."

Alice noticed that Heather didn't have many other toys and that there was only one other dress in her closet. She also noticed that the house was not very warm and that the furniture was old and the curtains were torn.

But Heather was fun to play with, and her grandmother was nice.

Soon it was time for Alice to go. She said good-bye to Heather and hurried home. She told her mother about her new friend and about her cold house, her old doll, and her thin coat, and that she had no boots or gloves and didn't even have a mother or father. She liked Heather a lot, and she kept thinking and thinking about her.

Then she had an idea. "Mother, Heather's birthday is Saturday. I want to give her one of my dolls. She could have Susie—she's still as good as new. And she could have my blue coat. It's too small for me, but it would fit her. And Mother, you know that money I was saving for a bicycle? I can't ride a bike in the winter anyway. I could buy some boots and gloves for Heather. Maybe I could give her one of my dresses, too, if you could shorten it a little. I think she would look nice in the yellow one with the little flowers on it."

Her mother said, "Alice, I think that's a wonderful idea. We could wrap all the things up and leave them on Heather's porch. I think we should put in a gift for Heather's grandmother, too." Then Mother added, "Would you like to invite them to have dinner with us?"

"Oh, yes," answered Alice. "And let's not tell who the presents are from."

For the next few days, Alice and her mother shopped for boots and gloves and wrapped gifts. On Friday, after dark, they went to Heather's house. They quietly set the presents on the porch, knocked on the door, and then hurried away.

(Pause while the children experience the joy of imagining what happened next.)

When Heather and her grandmother came to Alice's house for dinner the next day, Heather was wearing a warm blue coat and new boots and gloves and holding a beautiful doll tightly in her arms. She said, "Oh, Alice, just see what I got for my birthday—and Grandma got a new sweater." Then Heather took off her coat, and under it she wore a pretty yellow dress with flowers on it.

Alice smiled and smiled. She felt so happy that she could hardly speak. "Oh, Heather," she exclaimed, "I'm glad you had such a lovely birthday."

(c) *Secret buddies.* Put the names of all family members in a hat and let each child draw one out. The person whose name he draws becomes his secret buddy. No one tells whose name he drew during the week. Each person looks for anonymous good deeds to do for his secret buddy (make his bed, shine his shoes, leave him a treat).

At the end of the week, each person tries to guess who his secret buddy was. Two prizes are given: one for the "secretest" (took most guesses to guess), and one for the "buddiest" (did the most things for his secret buddy).

(d) *Interest table.* Have a certain place in the home, preferably a table or shelf that is out of baby's reach, where family members can share interesting things they discover. The items displayed might be a snail shell, a bird's nest, a picture from a magazine, a new book, a letter from a friend—anything that a family member wants to share with the family.

2. *Adaptation of methods from previous chapters.*

(a) *Four-facet review.* As you think individually about each child each month, ponder his understanding of service and contributing. Look for ways to involve each in service.

(b) *Weekly sessions.* At least periodically, help each child make one of his weekly goals a service- or contribution-oriented goal.

(c) *Ancestor stories.* Look for any incident in your parents' or grandparents' lives that is related to contribution—someone who ran for office, who led a cause, who served well in the community or in a job. Tell the story periodically, emphasizing the genetic and environmental heredity that makes you and your children and that ancestor alike.

(d) *Reinforcement.* Positive reinforcement is a great key. When a child thinks in terms of helping others, when he makes any sort of contribution, praise him generously.

3. *Perspective.* (To help children see how fortunate they are compared to many other children in the world.)

Sponsoring a needy child in a third-world country is a way to acquaint children with how fortunate they are. Most sponsorship programs permit and translate correspondence so that your children can ask your sponsored child about his lifestyle. As your children become more acquainted with the sponsored child, they will want to contribute some of their own money and will receive new insights about their own circumstances.

As children began to study geography in school, it is fun to sit down with them and, using a world globe, talk about different parts of the world. Emphasize that many people are cold and hungry most of the time, and that since we have so much by comparison, we should be doing all we can to help others. *National Geographic, Smithsonian Magazine,* and similar publications picture other cultures and are helpful in heightening your children's appreciation of the beauties as well as the hardships of those cultures. The pictures and an accompanying discussion will help them realize how many advantages we have, and they will begin to grasp the responsibility that implies.

4. *Charity concert.* As discussed in chapter 8, a wonderful way to get children involved in contributing is to hold a neighborhood concert. The children perform, parents pay admission, and the money goes to needy children.

5. *Help a needy family.* There are, of course, many ways to assist others. Little children understand this kind of service better when it is personal. If possible, locate a family, learn the name, age, and sex of each child, and become involved with your children in selecting or finding special gifts for them.

6. "*What you'll be when you grow up.*" (To help children make contributing an important factor in their long-range goals and choices.)

Most children love to speculate about what they will be. Their choices usually are based on different criteria, according to age. Smaller children usually want to be something exciting and adventurous—a policeman, a fireman, an astronaut—or they want to become what father is or what mother is. As they get older, they are more inclined to base their choices on things like status or money. When real maturity and responsibility are introduced into their lives, they may be able to begin thinking of their future in terms of contributing.

When the subject comes up, add a little "rider" question to the discussion. After Jimmy says he wants to be a fireman, ask, "What could you do to help people if you were a fireman? There is a good and obvious answer, as there is with almost every legitimate career ideal. Help your child see that the first and most important reason for choosing a particular career is that you can contribute something to others.

7. *Making gifts of gifts.* (To help children see that the talents they possess can be *given* to others, that the result is happiness for both the giver and the receiver as well as further development of the gifts.)

Gather the children together and tell them that you are going to play an imagination game. On a large sheet of paper, make a list of each child's particular talents in large enough print that everyone can read the list when you hold it up.

Then say, "We are going to use our imaginations and pretend it is the future. We are going to pick one talent that belongs to someone here and imagine the most wonderful use we can think of for that talent—a way that it could contribute to the lives of others. Then we will see if anyone can guess which family member we are talking about."

For example, "I can see someone seated at the huge Steinway piano on the stage of Carnegie Hall. The house is packed. It is a benefit concert for the new school that is being built. Dignitaries and philanthropists have paid one hundred dollars a seat to hear the famous young pianist perform." And so forth. (The children raise their hands when they think they know which family member's "contributing-future" is being described.)

Another example: "I can see someone in a laboratory with some test tubes and stacks of note paper. He's trying something. It works! He thinks he has discovered a new approach for fighting cancer. He has spent the past eight years attacking this most perplexing medical problem of all time, and at last his work seems to be paying off. In his mind he imagines the thousands of cancer victims who will be saved from an early and tragic death." (Again, the children raise their hands when they know who is being discussed.)

Don't worry about being too extreme or exaggerated in your descriptions of what may happen to each child. Children usually know when they are engaged in imagination, and the higher you imagine them taking their gifts, the more likely it is that they will at least strive for their potential.

C. Family Focal Points: Family Flag and "Secret Service"

We have a family flag. We made it one summer to fly on the Fourth of July below the American flag. When it is not flying for some holiday or special event (which includes birthdays), it hangs on the wall of our family room. This flag is the key symbol in the institutionalization of our family. It looks something like this:

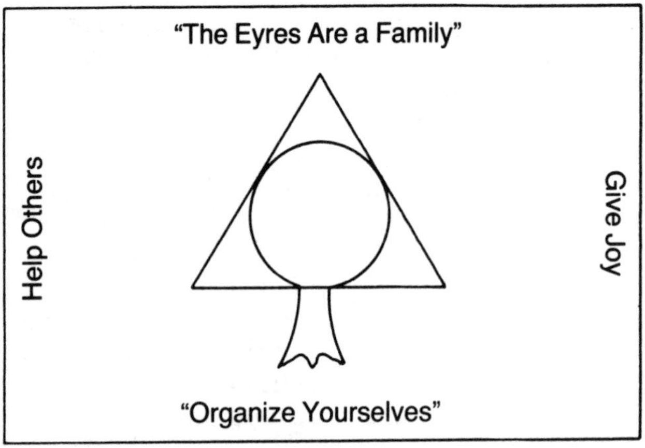

The triangle at the center symbolizes the three things we hold most dear: family, freedom, and faith. The tree symbol—a round tree with a trunk connecting to spreading roots—represents the children (branches), the parents (trunk), and our ancestors (roots), and reminds us that we are each other's first priority and that we have a noble heritage.

Around the border are the title of our family song ("The Eyres Are a Family," which we composed together several years ago), our family slogan (at the bottom), and our two family mottos (Help Others and Give Joy).

Almost everything on the flag, and particularly the mottos

and the slogan, emphasizes contribution. We try to focus the children's attention on the flag frequently and to ask ourselves, "How are we doing on our mottos? On our slogan? What more could we do on each? Who has some suggestions?" Each time we have that discussion, we think of someone to help or someone to whom we could bring a little joy. We feel that the exercise has a subconscious as well as conscious effect on the children, making it more natural for them to view life in a "contribution-opportunity" perspective.

During our weekly sessions, as we are planning the week ahead, one child (on a rotating basis) thinks of a "secret service," and act of service or sharing or a good deed that can be done anonymously for a neighbor or friend, sometimes even for a stranger. These have ranged from a bouquet of flowers for a newly moved-in neighbor to a major yard cleanup for someone who was out of town.

If the child whose turn it is that week can't think of an appropiate "secret service," we discuss it as a family and come up with something. Then it is written (or drawn) on a piece of paper and takes its place on the wall. We decide which day we will do the service, and we make a notation on the family monthly calendar that hangs on the same wall.

It is interesting how difficult it is at first for children to think of things to do for others. Their minds tend to function in a self-centered way, and they are infinitely more aware of their own needs than of others' needs. Coming up with a "secret service" each week helps to alter the selfish thought patterns that are so natural to us all.

To further motivate unselfish thinking, we offer the children a "daddy date" or "mommy date" anytime they think of a good service idea that can be done by themselves and one parent.

Section 4 Summary Story

As the Thompson family finished this book and spent a month focusing on responsibility for smaller children and another month each on dependability and on contribution, Dan and Corry began to realize that this final section was the key to the implementation of all the rest of the book. They realized this because they saw how much their two older children were able to influence and help the two younger ones. With the help of the older children—with their being part of the solution rather than part of the problem—Dan and Corry felt that it was possible to keep some effective emphasis on all the forms of responsibility. The older children would provide the example as well as much of the day-to-day teaching of the smaller ones.

This realization also looked like a solution to another concern that had come up with the Thompsonville Family Bank. The two younger children were not able to comprehend the value of money or the notion of checkbooks, nor could they remember to turn in their daily slips as the older ones could. By using the two older children as sort of "middle management," Dan and Corry felt that they could give them a new dimension of responsibility *and* find a way to involve the little ones more effectively in the responsibility system. What they did was this:

1. In a complimentary and flattering way, they assigned each of the two older children to be the *tutor* of one of the two younger ones. They explained that it was a one-month assignment and then they would trade with each other. They discussed what tutoring involved: helping the younger one to get his pegs in (see pages 55–57), to keep the family laws, and to reach his weekly goals.
2. They revised the Thomsponville Family Bank "point" system (see pages 59–60) so that only the older children turned in daily slips. The points were revised so that in addition to the 50 points already possible, a tutor would receive 5 points for each of his student's four pegs that was properly put in. Thus, the older children could get 70 points each day. The system was changed so that 300 points over the five weekdays caused the total to double. The net effect was that the tutors could not get their points doubled unless they had the help (and the points) of their students. At the end of the week, when the tutors got their pay, they each wrote out a check for 20 percent of the amount to their respective student.

The system took much of the responsibility off of Dan and Corry and give it to the older children, teaching them both the joy and the challenge of being "in charge" of someone else. It also gave the smaller ones a clear example to follow in their older siblings.

Postscript: Starting a "TCR" School in Your Home

Some readers will use this book simply by reading it and applying its principles daily. Others will try hard to work on a single form of responsibility each month. Still others will want a more structured and disciplined way to teach responsibility. This section is for those in the third category.

Let us share with you portions of an article we wrote some time ago for a magazine. Then let us tell you of a way you can supplement your children's elementary education and at the same time teach them the principles of responsibility.

Supplementing Your Child's Public Education

Fact #1: We're all grateful for public education.
Fact #2: None of us are fully satisfied with it.

So what do we (as parents) do? Some of us do nothing but grumble. We wish the schools would emphasize writing more (and all communication skills . . . reading, speaking, listening). We wish they would expose our children more thoroughly to the arts and to the classics. We wish there was more emphasis on individual creativity. We wish there was a little less premium on giving "right answers" and playing academic games and a little more premium on asking good questions and on the love of learning itself. We wish all of these things, but we don't know what to do about them, so we do nothing.

Others among us are at the other extreme. Instead of doing nothing, they do everything. They take their children right out of public schools and teach them themselves, in their homes. Others struggle to afford private education and often find the same inadequacies there that they found in public schools.

But many of us are looking for a more practical and more affordable middle ground! We feel that there are some voids in our children's education, some areas of incompleteness, some crucial skills that need more emphasis. We feel strongly enough that we don't want to sit back and do nothing. We want to have more input and control over what our children learn . . . yet it may be too expensive to try private schools, too impractical to start full-fledged "home schools" in our homes, and too late to lobby through school boards and PTAs to change the public schools. Perhaps, because it is the only solution left, we find ourselves in agreement with essayist Wendell Berry, who says: "If public education is to have any meaning or value at all, then public education must be supplemented by home education."

The word *supplement* is the key. Accept the many fine and even remarkable aspects of public education . . . with gratitude. But be aware of what your children are *not* learning there. And supplement their education in your home.

Here is a specific set of suggestions for how to do so:

1. Get your whole family, especially the children in elementary school, together for dinner at least three times a week.

2. On Mondays, go around the table and have each person (parents included) speak extemporaneously for sixty seconds on a confined topic. Have each speaker stand, give him his topic ("pebbles," "milk," "the color red," etc.), let him think for fifteen seconds, and then start the one-minute timer. Look for the good and praise it. Teach by your own example. During the remainder of the dinner hour, play some form of selected music and talk about it together.

3. On Wednesdays play "the question game" while you eat. Present the children with a topic and give them sixty seconds to come up with the best question they can about it. The tougher the question is the better. Discuss the questions. Look up answers in the encyclopedia after dinner.

4. On Fridays, call the children to the table fifteen minutes before dinner is served and have them write something (a short theme, a poem, or whatever you assign on a given topic). Encourage the use of new words. Let them read their papers to the family at dinner. Finish the dinner hour by reading to them an excerpt from classic literature of your choice.

We were amazed at the public response to the article. We began to realize how many parents felt the same dilemma we did—of wanting to keep their children in public schools but not wanting their education and potential to suffer.

Most of the responses we received from the article went something like this: "Yes, we agree, and we *want* to supplement our children's education, and a dinner time session two or three times a week probably is practical. But help us, because we don't have the materials or the teaching methods to do it!"

About the same time, we began to hear from the members of our TCJ * parenting organization. They were just receiving the first copies of the first edition of *Teaching Your Children Responsibility*. They were involved in neighborhood coopera-

---

*TCJ stands for "Teaching Children Joy." See the response card at the end of the book.

tive "joy schools" for their preschoolers and wanted to know if anything similar could be done for their elementary-age children under the auspices of *Teaching Your Children Responsibility*.

We became convinced that active, concerned parents all across the country wanted to do two complementary things with their elementary-age chilren:

1. Teach them responsibility.
2. Supplement their education in areas where public schools don't do an adequate job.

So we established TCR. TCR is a straightforward, month-to-month program through which individual homes and neighborhoods become supplemental learning institutions with parents teaching children the principles of communication, creativity, questions and research, goal setting, and planning. In TCR each of these skills is taught to children in the context of accepting responsibility. Through the national TCR co-op, a family receives a lesson-plan manual, a newsletter, and an audio music and discussion tape each month. With these materials, the parents conduct brief dinnertime sessions with their children in which certain academic skills are used and practiced as the "responsibility of the month" is being discussed. For example, if the month's focus was *"Responsibility for Choices,"* Monday night's extemporaneous sixty-second speeches would be on topics having to do with decisions and alternatives. Wednesday night's "question game" would be based on categories having to do with choices and methods of decision-making, and Friday night's writing would have the subject matter of situations calling for good choices.

Give it a try in your own home. If you feel that you can develop you own curriculum or supplemental lesson plan materials for your children, *do it.* If you'd like some help, write for information to TCR, 1615 Foothill Drive, Salt Lake City, Utah 84108; or call (801) 581-0112.

Index

To obtain a free catalog of HOMEBASE parenting and family programs, and an overview audio tape by Linda and Richard Eyre, send the card below, along with $5.00 for postage and handling, to:

HOMEBASE
1615 South Foothill Drive
Salt Lake City, UT 84108

Or call (801) 581-0112.

HOMEBASE
WORLD-WIDE

. . . is an international co-op of parents dedicated to making children and family their first priority and to the fostering of traditional values and correct principles in all of our institutions and in society at large.

For preschoolers "TCJ" (Teaching Children Joy) or "Joy Schools" - In-home, do-it-yourself neighborhood preschools focusing on the physical, mental and social "joys" of childhood.

For elementary age children "TCR" (Teaching Children Responsibility) - A program (stories, discussions, music) to conduct around the dinner table that teaches all forms of responsibility and self reliance.

For all ages but particularly adolescents "TCV" (Teaching Children Values) - A once-a-week Sunday program — materials and audio tapes to teach sensitivity, honesty and other values.

For busy parents "LFB" (Lifebalance) - A video and audio tape seminar with fill-in-the blank materials on how to balance family, work and personal needs.

Yes! I am interested in the possibility of membership in HOMEBASE. Please send me further information about:

❑ **TCJ** ❑ **TCV**
❑ **TCR** ❑ **LFB**

Name ______________________ Phone ______________________
(area code / number)

Address ______________________ ______________________
(street) (city / state / zip)